Suffer *the* Children

ALSO BY MARILYN WEDGE

In the Therapist's Mirror:
Reality in the Making

Suffer *the* Children

THE CASE AGAINST LABELING AND MEDICATING

AND AN EFFECTIVE ALTERNATIVE

MARILYN WEDGE

W. W. NORTON & COMPANY

New York   London

For information about permission to reproduce selections from this book,
write to Permissions, W. W. Norton & Company, Inc.,
500 Fifth Avenue, New York, NY 10110

For information about special discounts for bulk purchases, please contact
W. W. Norton Special Sales at specialsales@wwnorton.com or 800-233-4830

Manufacturing by RR Donnelley, Harrisonburg
Book design by Amanda Dewey
Production manager: Julia Druskin

Library of Congress Cataloging-in-Publication Data

Wedge, Marilyn.
Suffer the children : the case against labeling and medicating and an effective
alternative / Marilyn Wedge.—1st ed.
p. ; cm.
Includes bibliographical references and index.
ISBN 978-0-393-07159-7 (hardcover)
1. Child psychotherapy. 2. Family psychotherapy. I. Title.
[DNLM: 1. Child Behavior Disorders—therapy. 2. Attention Deficit and Disruptive
Behavior Disorders—therapy. 3. Child Psychiatry—trends. 4. Child. 5. Family Therapy
—methods. 6. Psychotropic Drugs—adverse effects. 7. Unnecessary Procedures—
trends. WS 350.6]
RJ504.W34 2011
618.92'8914—dc22

2010041045

W. W. Norton & Company, Inc.
500 Fifth Avenue, New York, N.Y. 10110
www.wwnorton.com

W. W. Norton & Company Ltd.
Castle House, 75/76 Wells Street, London W1T 3QT

1 2 3 4 5 6 7 8 9 0

For my parents,

FAYE AND EDWARD WELTZ

In loving memory

Contents

CONTENTS

Suffer *the* Children

Do No Harm

THIS BOOK WAS BORN on an unseasonably cool evening in January 2009. My day had been especially busy—besides my usual clients I had appointments with three families that I was seeing for the first time. I'd barely had time to grab a quick lunch.

As a family therapist, I view the family as the unit for therapy. This doesn't mean that the entire family comes to every session. At any given time, I might see a mother and son, two parents and their children, a teenager by herself, and even parents without their kids. I have worked with families for more than twenty years, resolving children's problems, usually in fewer than seven sessions, and helping families heal themselves. It has been a rewarding career, and I am grateful that I have been able to help so many families regain their equilibrium and see their children triumph over seemingly insurmountable obstacles.

On this particular day, the new families had been referred by school counselors in my small community. One child was a second grader who couldn't sit still in the classroom, and the counselor thought he might have attention-deficit hyperactivity disorder (ADHD). Another was a girl of ten who had such severe mood swings that the counselor, as well as the girl's frantic parents, feared she might be bipolar. The third was an adolescent boy who told me he had nothing to look forward to in life and wanted to die.

I have treated many children with symptoms like these—and worse. But what struck me that evening, as I sat down with a cup of tea to review my notes, was that before they came to see me, all the parents had taken their child to a psychiatrist, on the school's recommendation, and each psychiatrist had advised that the youngster be given medication.

I was dismayed. Of course, I'm no stranger to children's worrisome behaviors. But instead of giving them a label or a diagnosis, I view children's symptoms—unhappiness, jumpiness, moodiness, suicidal thoughts—not as signs of a "psychiatric disorder" but as evidence of something wrong in the family, something that I can remedy with the right interventions.

Most parents in my practice have been anxious to avoid medicating their children. But as I was reviewing my notes that evening, a chilling thought occurred to me. I realized that in the past few months I had been seeing more and more children like the ones in my office that day, children who were already tagged as bipolar or depressed or hyperactive—even autistic. More children were coming to me already taking medication, some of them so heavily dosed that they seemed more like sedated little adults than active children.

Why was this so? I asked myself. Why were so many youngsters taking psychiatric medications (or being told to do so) and why was the number of children coming to therapy skyrocketing? My intuition told me that the answers to these questions had something to do with our society's values, and I pondered what influences were at work beneath the surge of childhood psychiatric diagnoses.

Some years earlier, I wrote a book about my method of child-focused family therapy that was aimed at my peers—clinicians and researchers in family therapy. The book was well received, but it did not carry its message to the broader audience of parents and teachers. Now, confronting a burgeoning epidemic of children's emotional and behavioral problems, accompanied by a disturbing "quick-fix" response from the psychiatric community, I decided it was time to draw on my clinical experience and knowledge of child and family development to offer an alternative form of treatment. Thus, I began to write *Suffer the Children*.

At first I thought that the epidemic of children's problems had something to do with life in California, the state in which I live and practice. California has a soaring divorce rate, even higher than that of the rest of the country. Our schools are underfunded and over-crowded compared to those in many other states. Social isolation is another serious problem in California, as many nuclear families lack the support of their extended families, which often live thousands of miles away. Many children here grow up barely knowing grandparents, aunts, uncles, and cousins. Also, because the cost of living in California is relatively high, more families need two incomes to make ends meet. With both parents working, children spend long hours in day care after school. All these factors could certainly put more stress on children.

But therapists in other parts of the country were telling me that they were seeing the same thing: a striking rise in children's emotional and behavioral problems; a startling upsurge in the diagnoses of ADHD, childhood depression, autism, and bipolar disorder; and a noticeable increase in the number of young children taking psychiatric medications. The children's mental health epidemic appeared to be nationwide.

As I began to look closely at the facts, the story became even grimmer. More than four and a half million children in the United States have been diagnosed with ADHD. The number of children diagnosed with bipolar disorder is also exploding; by 2009, more than one million youngsters had been labeled with this serious affliction, which in the past had been thought to strike only adults. Taking a child to a psychiatrist for med checks was becoming as socially acceptable as taking a boy or a girl to basketball practice or dance class. It was just one more stop on a soccer mom's hectic driving schedule.

Yet, despite the social acceptability of medicating children who were inattentive or difficult to manage, many observers were raising questions about whether psychiatric drugs were really safe for children, especially in cases where the medications had not been tested and approved for pediatric use.

I don't know exactly when I first heard the term "Big Pharma," but suddenly I was hearing it everywhere. I began to suspect that powerful economic forces were driving the children's psychiatric epidemic. Developing new drugs, or re-purposing old ones and prescribing them to children, has been immensely profitable to drug companies and to the scores of psychiatrists and medical researchers who accept financial perks from the pharmaceutical industry. So potent are these medications that some of them must be labeled with a "black box," a warning that the medication might have terrible side effects on children. Even more surprising to me, child psychiatrists were prescribing drugs to children without accompanying the treatment with any form of therapy or counseling. I began to wonder if child psychiatry was collectively going mad.

I was not alone in having these thoughts. Other family therapists were as dismayed as I was about reports that child psychiatrists were giving cocktails of psychotropic drugs to children as young as two years old. Even from within the field of psychiatry itself, doctors were beginning to question the very sanity of their profession. Many courageous psychiatrists were voicing their concerns that biological child psychiatry, which relies heavily on pharmacological treatment, was not a genuine science at all. These concerned doctors pointed out that psychiatrists and medical researchers were colluding with pharmaceutical companies to weave a web of childhood psychiatric diagnoses that, like the emperor's new clothes, may not be what they seem. Certainly some children are more active and impulsive than others and some are exceptionally irritable and moody. But to posit that a child can have bipolar disorder from the minute he is born—as some psychiatrists have claimed—is to ignore entirely the influence of the child's family environment.

Medical science has made impressive and worthy advances in recent decades, and most people tend to put their faith in the judgment of doctors. So it is no surprise that the American public doesn't think to question what is happening in child psychiatry. But shouldn't we be questioning what psychiatry is saying about our children's troubles and how to fix them, especially if it conflicts with the most ordinary dictates of common sense? Doesn't the mind boggle at the notion of giving two-year-olds antipsychotic drugs meant for adults? Doesn't common sense balk at the idea of a teenager taking Zoloft or Prozac, drugs that have been associated with suicide in young people? Most of us have known children who were a little odd or defiant or impulsive, without concluding that their differentness is a sign of a psychiatric disorder. Do we really believe there is no better way to help these children conform to our expectations than to brand them with a psychiatric label and insist they take drugs to "cure their mental illness"?

As I thought more deeply about these dilemmas, I couldn't help but think that what might appear as "crazy" behavior in a grown person—tantrums, impulsiveness, a short attention span—is often business as usual in a child. Similarly, for a child to believe in Santa Claus does not suggest a delusional disorder. But if we see an adult waiting eagerly on Christmas Eve for a bearded man in a sleigh pulled by flying reindeer, we might think about calling 911.

There is no doubt that pharmaceutical treatment has helped millions of seriously disturbed adults lead normal lives; but when it comes to children, there is no indication at all that either the diagnoses or treatments that work for adults apply to kids. Moreover, as I show in the chapters that follow, since the turn of the twentieth century, alarming evidence has accumulated that psychiatric drugs hold real dangers for children, including hallucinations, abnormal breast growth in boys, weight gain, and cardiovascular problems.

At the far end of the spectrum of side effects, some children have tragically lost their lives as a result of psychiatric medication. This was the case with four-year-old Rebecca Riley, who was diagnosed with bipolar disorder before her third birthday and given a cocktail of three powerful psychiatric medications. Rebecca died on December 13, 2006, from an overdose of clonidine, one of the three drugs that she was taking. Both of her parents were later convicted of murder. What struck me most about Rebecca's story, which was reported on *60 Minutes*, was that her psychiatrist treated her only with medication and did not recommend any form of counseling for Rebecca or her family. As difficult as it was for me to understand why Rebecca's psychiatrist did not recommend family counseling, I have come to realize that more and more parents in our society rely on a psychiatric diagnosis and medication for their troubled children without turning to counseling or therapy.

I have no doubt that parents who bring their children to psychiatrists have only good intentions. They want their sons and daughters to have the best chance of succeeding in school and in life. If a psychiatric diagnosis and medication help a child become less fidgety and more focused in the classroom, or less oppositional and moody at home, I can certainly understand how parents are willing to accept this route.

Sadly, though, it seems to me that parents are so pressured by the need to see their child at the top of the class and en route to the Ivy League that they sometimes take leave of their own good common sense. Parents today seem more distraught than the mothers and fathers I've seen in the past. Often, because teachers are so concerned about school performance, parents are anxious to resolve their kids' problems immediately and to set their children on a "normal" path. They are thus more willing to embrace psychiatry's nostrums for their "mentally ill" children. This state of affairs is, I believe, at the heart of today's crisis in child mental health.

In this book I explore how we as parents, as health professionals, and as a society can best help our country's children weather the crisis. I present my "secret weapon" for tackling even the most daunting of children's problems in a safe and benevolent way. My secret weapon is family therapy—specifically child-focused family therapy, the variation that I have developed in my two decades of working with children and families.

My approach includes meeting not only with a child's parents, siblings, and at times their extended family, but also with teachers, school psychologists, and counselors. I have developed creative strategies to help children cope with stress or sadness, school problems or aggressiveness, anxiety or compulsive behaviors. I have taught mothers and fathers (and sometimes even grandparents) new techniques of parenting and new ways of communicating that have helped countless families I've worked with over the years. I share these successful strategies throughout the book, and I am confident that you will learn from them and be inspired to apply these principles to your own family.

Here you will find true stories of children who are aggressive, explosive, inattentive, depressed, or even suicidal. You will meet four-year-old Joey, who held a knife to his throat and threatened to kill himself, and eight-year-old Cora, who began failing at school for no apparent reason. You will get to know Elizabeth, who washed her hands compulsively, and Jarrod, who hit and bit other children. And you will hear about eleven-year-old Brian, an Australian boy who was diagnosed with depression and school phobia, and whose problems

I succeeded in resolving long-distance just by giving his parents a simple list of directives.

You will also encounter some of the pioneering sages of family therapy—Jay Haley, Milton Erickson, and Salvador Minuchin—who dared to envision a brand-new way of treating the troubles that bring parents and children to therapy and who left us a rich legacy of ideas and techniques for overcoming children's problems.

All the stories in this book are true, although details and names are changed to preserve anonymity. My hope is that you will recognize aspects of your own family in the stories and will gain a richer understanding of how parents and children can rise above their tribulations and become happier. I am confident that the therapeutic strategies I bring to life on these pages will empower you to deal with the most thorny of problems, the most difficult of challenges. My goal is always to help families help themselves without the use of drugs or stigmatizing diagnoses.

Family therapy is not a magic bullet, nor is it a prolonged course of "talk therapy." Rather, it is a holistic and humanistic approach to treatment that frames a child's problem in the wider context of the family. Some of the strategies come from ordinary common sense. Others are more sophisticated and paradoxical. All are intended to treat children—even those with the most serious disturbances—without diagnosing them with mental disorders and without using drugs to control them. The techniques are easy to understand and easy to put into action. Most important, you can use them without reservations or fear because, unlike psychiatric medications, they can do no harm.

Before I unveil how family therapy can help parents and children overcome overwhelming difficulties, let's take a closer look at how child psychopharmacology ascended to the top of the therapeutic ladder, and why I believe it is imperative that parents and professionals adopt a new, more humane approach to children's emotional and behavioral problems.

ONE

Beyond Psychiatric Labels

What Stories Tell Us

I N 2008, AN ARTICLE in the *New York Times Magazine* chronicled a shocking saga of a little boy named James. When James was only four, he was given the label "oppositional defiant disorder" after his preschool told his parents that he was hyperactive and aggressive in the classroom. A developmental pediatrician prescribed the antidepressant Zoloft for James; but his parents refused to give it to him, believing that a four-year-old boy was too young for such a potent drug.

As James struggled through the school year, his parents took him to a pediatric psychopharmacologist, who prescribed Risperdal, a new-generation antipsychotic drug. Although his anger seemed to decrease while he was taking Risperdal, James started to have attention problems at school. His parents consulted another doctor, who diagnosed James with ADHD and prescribed two stimulant drugs. James's out-of-control behavior still did not improve. He became even more aggressive and angry, and life at home became a nightmare.

Eventually, this unfortunate little boy was given Depakote, an antiseizure drug also used to treat bipolar disorder. Ultimately, the Depakote was replaced with Lamictal, another antiseizure drug, and the Risperdal was replaced with Abilify, another antipsychotic. Finally, when James was eight, a psychiatrist diagnosed him with bipolar disorder, and James began taking lithium, a mood-stabilizing medication frequently prescribed for adults but rarely for children. Tragically, none of these potentially dangerous drugs—drugs that had not been tested for long-term toxic effects on children—helped James. His psychiatrist then suggested that his parents put him in a residential facility.

To any reasonable person, a story like this sounds more like mayhem than medicine. The *New York Times Magazine* reporter did not say much about James's family life, but the article suggests that his parents were well meaning and well educated and not at all abusive. Why did these parents resort to extreme pharmacological remedies for their son's disturbing behavior? Why did none of the well-respected physicians they consulted suggest an alternative approach such as counseling, even as his parents became more and more desperate when one medication after another failed to help their son? To address these questions, we need to look at the complex changes that have sparked a revolution in the field of child psychiatry since the 1970s.

At the hot center of this revolution is the runaway growth of the alliance between pharmaceutical companies and psychiatric researchers. With studies aggressively financed and promoted by drug companies—and disseminated to the clinical community as "received wisdom"—most psychiatrists and other professionals have swallowed whole the notion that drugs offer the best hope for "curing" children's psychological problems. It is no surprise that professionals have passed this outlook on to parents. Often, in fact, parents themselves request medication for their children, thanks to the drug industry's robust consumer advertising.

Psychiatrists are paid a great deal of money by drug companies to carry forth the message that children's emotional and behavioral problems are symptoms of brain disease. Dr. Joseph Biederman, of Harvard University Medical School, earned at least $1.6 million in consulting fees from drug companies between the years 2000 and 2007. Colleagues of Dr. Biederman also received more than $1 million from drug companies during the same period.

Many experts, including California pediatrician Lawrence Diller, author of *Running on Ritalin,* argue that these psychiatrists are diagnosing children with mental illnesses that require drug treatment for no sound medical reason, but rather to reap personal gain from drug companies.

In an article entitled "Misguided Standards of Care," published in the *Boston Globe* on June 19, 2007, Diller holds Biederman and his colleagues to be in part "morally responsible" for the death of Rebecca Riley because they provided so-called "scientific" justification for treating her with drugs.

Some observers even think that Biederman single-handedly created the social epidemics of ADHD and bipolar disorder that are plaguing our country's children. On November 24, 2008, *New York Times* journalist Gardiner Harris reported that "Dr. Biederman's work helped to fuel a fortyfold increase from 1994 to 2003 in the diagnosis of pediatric bipolar disorder and a rapid rise in the use of powerful, risky and expensive antipsychotic medicines in children."

The risk of these drugs has been amply documented. The largest study so far of the use of antipsychotic drugs, including Risperdal and Abilify, on children and adolescents produced ominous findings. Two hundred fifty-seven children and youth with mood and behavior problems who were taking these drugs for the first time rapidly gained a significant amount of weight and had increased blood levels of cholesterol or triglycerides. The study's findings were published in the *Journal of the American Medical Association* on October 28, 2009.

In an accompanying editorial, physicians Christopher Varley and Jon McClellan of Seattle Children's Hospital said that "given the risk for weight gain and long-term risk for cardiovascular and metabolic problems, the widespread and increasing use of atypical antipsychotic medications in children and adolescents should be reconsidered." Children and teenagers under nineteen years old accounted for 15 percent of antipsychotic drug use in 2005, a dramatic increase from 7 percent in 1996.

In a study by the U.S. Food and Drug Administration (FDA), published in the journal *Pediatrics* in February 2009, researchers found that drugs commonly used to treat ADHD and attention-deficit disorder (ADD) caused symptoms of psychosis and mania in children. The drugs in the study included Ritalin, Adderall XR, Concerta, and Strattera. The study concluded that for every hundred children who take ADHD drugs for a year, one or two will experience a drug-related psychotic event. If we consider that between two and four million children in this country are taking the medications in this study, the number of children who will experience side effects, including hallucinations and mania, is shocking. A greater concern is that doctors might not recognize that a child's psychotic symptoms are actually a *result* of being treated with the drugs, and not symptoms that sprang from a different cause.

It is important to note that many of the charges against pediatric drugs are aimed at the makers of drugs intended for adults, not children. To take but one example: In 2009, the Justice Department filed a civil complaint against drug maker Forest Laboratories, alleging that Forest concealed a clinical study that showed that two of its best-selling antidepressant drugs, Lexapro and Celexa—customarily prescribed for adults—were not effective in children and might even cause children to become suicidal. Even more alarming than concealing negative research results is the fact that some drug makers have resorted to intimidation of medical students and blacklisting of psychiatrists who challenge the psychopharmacological approach.

The ties between medical researchers and private industry are a serious cause for public concern and cast doubt on whether pharmaceutically oriented child psychiatry is entitled to be called genuine science at all. In fact, the very term "mental illness" is misleading because it is based on a parallel between psychological problems and physical illness. To put human suffering and emotional pain in the same category as biological illness is to use language metaphorically. No pathogen has been identified as the cause of ADHD or bipolar disorder. No one has found the gene responsible for these conditions, although the search for genetic explanations continues to be well-funded.

With the diagnosing of mental disorders, there is not the same kind of consensus among physicians as there is with physical disease. Psychiatric diagnoses are subjective. As we saw in the story of James, one doctor may diagnose a child with ADHD or oppositional defiant disorder (ODD) and another might diagnose that same child with bipolar disorder. At present, no laboratory tests exist to confirm that a child has one of these disorders, and there is no consensus on the theory that they are caused by a chemical imbalance in the child's brain. Unlike biological diseases in other branches of medicine, psychiatric disorders are not classified according to causes.

The statement that a child has a mental disorder can be seen more as a spin than a statement of fact. It is the expression of a subjective position, not a medical certainty. We accept the idea that politicians disguise spins as facts all the time. They may use the word "fetus" or "baby," "pro-choice" or "pro-life," depending on the attitude toward abortion they want the public to accept. Thinking about aborting a fetus is much less emotionally charged than the idea of aborting a baby. So the phrase "ending the life of a baby" is a pro-life spin intended to persuade the public.

In the same vein, a family therapist might describe a child's misbehavior as "annoying" or "mischievous" or "disruptive." A family therapist would set up a behavioral program with the child's parents and his teacher. A child psychiatrist may diagnose the behavior as a symptom of ADHD and prescribe medication. These are two different ways of describing or spinning the same behavior. The difference is that a doctor's pronouncement that a child has a psychiatric disorder is chilling to a mother's heart and could easily persuade her that drug treatment is the only choice.

The thorny subject of diagnosis points to another reason why James's parents and many others like them do not think to question the clinicians treating their children. Diagnosis is a powerful concept. When a respected professional says, "Your son has ADHD" or "Your daughter has bipolar disorder," parents are not likely to challenge these statements any more than they would challenge a doctor's diagnosis of childhood diabetes.

Olympic world record gold medalist Michael Phelps was diagnosed with ADHD when he was in sixth grade. In his book *No Limits*, Phelps recalls that he felt embarrassed when he had to go to the nurse to get his lunchtime dose of Ritalin. If he forgot to go to her office, the nurse would come and get him in class. This was humiliating for Phelps, especially since he was already picked on by the other students.

At age thirteen, Phelps decided that he didn't want to take Ritalin anymore, even though he knew that it made him less "jumpy" in the classroom. He felt that the drug was an "unnecessary crutch" and that his mind was strong enough for him to succeed without medication. His family doctor respected his decision and gradually weaned Phelps off Ritalin. His mother, however, was skeptical that her son would be able to manage at school without medication. His teacher had told her he would never be successful because he couldn't concentrate on anything long enough.

But once Phelps had made his decision and set goals to control his classroom behavior and focus on his schoolwork, he found that he was up to the challenge. In an interview, Phelps said, "Your mind is the strongest medicine you can have . . .You can overcome anything if you think you can and you want to." Phelps added that he dealt with his aggressive feelings by swimming vigorously. In using swimming as an outlet for his extra energy and angry feelings, Phelps discovered for himself an intervention that every family therapist uses with children who have ADHD-like symptoms. We recommend that parents involve their child in soccer, tennis, softball, basketball, swimming, gymnastics, or any other sport that their child is interested in as an outlet for his or her extra energy.

Diagnoses like the one Michael Phelps received can even become self-fulfilling prophecies. If a child is branded with the label of ADHD, parents, teachers, doctors, and other family members will actually come to "see" that child as having ADHD. Like Phelps's mother, they will expect that the child needs medication to control his behavior because they think he has a chemical imbalance or some such biologically based defect. The child himself will come to believe that he has a "problem." Phelps was exceptional in that he had the self-confidence and skill to take control of his behavior and shake off the label of ADHD—which of course he could not have done if his problem was truly a biologically based disease. He also had the great gift of athletic talent to help him along.

Many young people are not as fortunate. If children are led to believe that their jumpiness or distractibility is a disease, they may not be motivated even to try to control their behavior by themselves. They may come to rely instead on their daily doses of medication. And there is new evidence from neurobiology suggesting that long-term use of psychostimulant drugs may actually suppress kids' motivation to act independently. The nucleus accumbens is the part of the brain associated with motivation to act. Recent research with laboratory animals suggests that regular use of psychostimulants like Ritalin may impair the functioning of this vital center of motivation. When juvenile rats were given stimulant medications of the kind used for ADHD in children, they displayed a loss of motivation and drive when they grew up.

In talking about the perils of labeling and diagnosis, I do not mean to suggest that distractibility, aggressiveness, anxiety, rebelliousness, and so forth do not exist. Rather, these are childhood behaviors that make parents, teachers, and other adults uncomfortable and impatient. They are not usually signs of a brain disease. They are more productively viewed as indications of troubled relationships in the child's world.

Although Phelps's mother worried that he would not be able to control his behavior without drugs, she apparently wasn't worried about the side effects of Ritalin. Parents' reliance on their doctors and on trusted drug companies—a trust fueled by consumer advertising—explains why parents are not always fully aware of the downside of drugs. Although some medications used for ADHD, such as Adderal XR, bear labels warning about side effects, including hallucinations, many parents and even pediatricians don't always take these warnings seriously. Some side effects do not even appear as "warnings" and are instead buried under a long list of "precautions." This was the case with the abnormal and irreversible breast growth that recently occurred in more than forty boys in clinical trials for the drug Risperdal, which doctors prescribed for their ADHD.

To be sure, many parents have had positive experiences with antidepressants and other psychiatric drugs in their own lives, and are understandably willing to try them with their children. In fact, parents have become so comfortable with pediatric psychiatric medications that they think of them in the same category as allergy pills. I've noticed, too, that some parents have abandoned commonsense words for ordinary childhood problems. Instead of telling me, "My son is too free-spirited and adventurous to do well at school," parents say things like "My son doesn't do well at school because he has ADHD."

Psychiatric drugs have become daily fare not only at elementary schools across the country but also at children's summer camps. A *New York Times* article in 2006 reported that between a quarter and half of the children at any given residential summer camp take psychiatric medications. This trend is bolstered by school pressure to "fix" children who misbehave in the classroom or who seem moody or withdrawn or out of control. James's preschool teachers told his parents that he was hyperactive and aggressive. Michael Phelps's teacher predicted he would never succeed. What mother and father wouldn't want to help their child make a better adjustment to the demands of the classroom?

Consider, finally, the "scientific evidence" for a biological cause of children's psychological problems. How do we account for the magnetic resonance imaging (MRI) scans that show in vivid color how the brains of "mentally ill" children differ from the brains of other children? This research is impressive, but framing a child's behavior problems as a brain disease leaves out an important observation. A child may be troubled only at school but not at home or vice versa. If he is troubled only at school, what happens to his "brain disease" when he is at home or at a friend's house? If a kid with school problems behaves well at his grandparents' house, where he can focus for hours on an exciting video game, what happens to his brain disease when he spends a weekend at Grandma's house?

Parents whose children take Ritalin or another stimulant medication often argue that the drug has transformed their child's life almost miraculously. Their stories abound. From being unable to concentrate on anything, a ten-year-old boy is now attentive and focused. From being slow to make decisions, a middle-school girl now makes choices quickly. Ritalin has eased these children's suffering and increased their self-esteem. My answer is that of course stimulant medications will help a fidgety child focus better. Amphetamine-type drugs like Ritalin will help *just about anyone* focus better, as many college students discover around final exam time when amphetamines, or "speed" drugs, are passed around college campuses like M&M's.

There is no question that Ritalin's "success" is seductive, but I have found that there are serious problems—in addition to side effects—that may not show up right away. One of the most intriguing consequences I've discovered is that if the core family disturbance is not resolved, another child in the same family will eventually begin to have problems. I have seen this over and over again in families that have temporarily resolved one of their children's so-called ADHD with drugs, only to have another child in the family become depressed or disruptive later because the parents haven't dealt with the underlying family issues.

Then, too, parents are teaching the child to use drugs as a crutch, a dependency that may lead him or her to use drugs as an adolescent or a young adult to face life's normal difficulties. Another problem is that stimulant drugs may have even more serious side effects that have not yet been made public. Clinical trials revealing negative data about drugs are regularly concealed by drug companies and medical researchers.

The lure of psychiatric drugs is indeed commanding. But with the growing doubt about the scientific credibility of diagnosing children with psychiatric disorders and treating them with drugs, there is every reason for parents to consider an alternative. One important option is family therapy, a safe, well-tested, and effective approach to children's emotional and behavioral problems that has been around for five decades.

Family therapy emerged in the 1950s in the United States from three main influences: the social scientist Gregory Bateson's project on human communication, the emergence of systems theory, and the brilliant and idiosyncratic techniques of the psychiatrist Milton Erickson. The Bateson project placed therapy in the arena of human communication rather than in the realm of biological causality. Bateson and his colleagues focused on how social interactions and communication could affect a person's well-being.

Systems theory is based on cybernetics, the science of communication and control in living and nonliving systems, developed by scientists in the late 1940s. From systems theory, family therapists learned that each individual is a part of a number of larger social systems, and these systems play a part in a person's behavior just as much as his genetic, biological, and psychological characteristics. Each member of a system influences the other members of the system, and the system as a whole influences its members.

Until the 1950s, Freud's psychodynamic theory dominated the therapy scene in the United States. Psychotherapy concerned itself with the inner life of the individual—the psyche. The psychoanalyst analyzed and interpreted the individual's feelings, fantasies, and dreams to discover what was buried in his unconscious and how these unconscious factors influenced the person's behavior. Systems theory inspired early family therapists to challenge the status quo of psychodynamic theory. It raised the possibility that an individual's free will and unconscious motivations were not the only explanations for human behavior. People did what they did, at least in part, because of what other people did. The psyche, or mind, in this view, is shaped by social interactions. Systems theorists were so intent on dethroning the psychodynamic model that one early family therapist, Don Jackson, wrote a paper in 1956 arguing that the "individual" does not exist.

Some of the early pioneers of family therapy were psychiatrists, including Milton Erickson, Murray Bowen, and Salvador Minuchin. Although these doctors had been properly trained in medicine, they became interested in nonbiological explanations of human emotional and behavioral problems. They believed that even the most severe psychological problems could be treated without drugs. They reframed psychiatric problems as relationship problems. Instead of thinking in terms of unhappy individuals, they thought in terms of unhappy families.

Another important, though often unacknowledged, influence on family therapy was the humanistic "moral treatment" approach that began in England and France in the early nineteenth century. This was one of the first therapeutic traditions that looked for the sources of behavioral and emotional problems in the patient's life experience, such as family crises, financial losses, and disappointments in love.

Although family therapy originated in the United States, variations of it have been practiced for decades in Europe, Australia, and New Zealand. In fact, family therapy has been more widely adopted in the rest of the world than it has in the United States because other countries are less inclined to prescribe psychiatric medications to children. In Italy, especially, systems theory took root and flourished. The psychiatrist Mara Selvini Palazzoli and her colleagues founded the Milan School of family therapy, and they were very successful in treating serious problems like childhood schizophrenia, anorexia, and autism.

The power of family therapy to help a child comes from framing the child as a member of a larger system. The family therapist aims at changing the system of which the child is a part and thus producing positive change in the child's feelings and behavior. The family therapist looks for explanations of a child's misbehavior in family conflicts *outside* the child rather than in some sort of mental disorder *inside* the child. It is true that these kinds of explanations are more complicated and more difficult to understand than simple cause and effect explanations. But it is certainly reasonable to hypothesize that social situations can affect the brain in ways not yet fully understood. In fact, recent developments in social neuroscience indicate that synaptic connections in the brain are affected by social interactions. UCLA neuroscience researcher Daniel Siegel, MD, maintains that social relationships are irreducibly part of both the mind and the brain.

According to Siegel, therapy itself—the therapist-client interaction—produces physiological changes in the brain.

If theories about communication and systems constituted family therapy's intellectual roots, the psychiatrist Milton Erickson was its personal progenitor. The most eccentric and colorful figure in family therapy's early history, Erickson was committed to the idea that the therapist must actively take responsibility for changing his patients' lives. He believed that if a therapist sat back passively, he could not bring about change.

A central organizing concept of the early family therapists was the notion of *hierarchy* in families. Parents are the adults in the family; they are in charge of their children just as managers are in charge of their subordinates. Family therapists found that when this hierarchy goes awry, a child will start to misbehave. For example, if parents disagree with each other about the rules of the house and how to discipline their child, the child, sensing this division, will likely misbehave and test the rules. If a child knows that Mommy and Daddy are divided on an issue, with one being strict and the other lenient, he will play one against the other and "comparison shop" between his parents to see where he will get the better deal.

Early family therapists found that if they intervened to get the parents to work as a team in enforcing consistent rules and consequences for their child, the child stopped acting out. Empowering parents to take charge of their children was one of the first successful strategies with all kinds of behavior problems of children and adolescents, from temper tantrums to drug abuse.

Another thing that can go wrong with a family hierarchy is that one parent, usually the mother, allies with a child against the other parent, making the child part of a triangular relationship. This undermining of the parent's authority can lead to serious problems. For example, in young people who use drugs, there is often a strong intergenerational alliance between the youth and his or her mother that disrupts the bond of the parents. In these cases, family therapists found that the most effective strategy to stop the drug use was to correct the family hierarchy, helping the parents to have a more loving relationship with each other so that neither parent had to ally with their child for emotional closeness.

In 1960, family therapist innovator Salvador Minuchin started to do therapy with whole families, mainly from low-income backgrounds. He published his results in the groundbreaking book *Families of the Slums*. In 1965, Minuchin, joined by his colleagues Braulio Montalvo, Bernice Rosman, and later Jay Haley, opened the Philadelphia Child Guidance Clinic in the heart of Philadelphia's black ghetto. There Minuchin trained hundreds of students in what he called structural family therapy. Ten years later, when Minuchin stepped down to pursue his interest in psychosomatic families, the clinic became part of a modern complex that included the Children's Hospital of Philadelphia.

Minuchin, too, was concerned with family hierarchy, but from a slightly different perspective. He talked about boundaries and subsystems within a family. For example, in a healthy family, parents form a system with an invisible boundary around them. They have private time together and go out on dates without their children. They do not allow a child to interrupt their conversations, unless the matter is urgent, or sleep with them in their bed. When parents allow a child to encroach on this boundary and engage too closely with a parent, the child begins to have problems. Structural family therapists found that correcting the boundaries between children and parents solved a wide variety of problems among children and adolescents.

Today there are many schools of family therapy—strategic, structural, narrative, and solution focused, among others—and they all have several things in common. They are, first, *brief therapies*. This means that family therapists are committed to solving problems in the fewest possible sessions—usually fewer than eight. The goal of resolving serious problems briefly was highly valued by early family therapists, in part because they worked with poor families who could not afford to pay for lengthy treatment.

All the variations of family therapy focus on the child's social context and include the child's family in the treatment. Usually social context means the parents, but, depending on the particular problem, siblings, grandparents, and even friends can be included in the sessions as well. Family therapy does not always mean assembling the child's whole family for every session. As we will see in later chapters, which family members are included depends on each individual case.

Family therapists also do not confine their efforts to the therapy office. They may talk with a child's teacher, school counselor, principal, grandparent, clergyperson, pediatrician, or anyone else in the child's world. This willingness to move outside the confines of the therapy office comes from the legacy of Milton Erickson. Ever unconventional and inventive, Erickson was not above making elevator operators, hairdressers, waiters, and his own family members participants in his efforts to help his patients. He even made house calls.

A mother once consulted Erickson about her fourteen-year-old daughter, who was becoming more and more withdrawn and socially isolated. She wouldn't even go to school or church. The girl was self-conscious because she thought her feet were too large. She would not talk to anyone about this, nor would she go to a doctor. Erickson, a master at maneuvering social situations, arranged with the mother for him to make a house call to examine the mother for the "flu." He went to the house, where the mother was "sick" in bed, and gave her a thorough physical examination.

During the examination, Erickson positioned himself so that the girl was directly behind him. Suddenly he stepped backward—coming down hard on the girl's toes. She of course squawked in pain. Erickson then shouted furiously at her that if her feet were large enough for a man to *see*, the accident wouldn't have happened. The girl was stunned to hear her mother's doctor yell at her because her feet were too small. That very same day, she asked to go out to a party. She soon returned to school and church, and participated in social activities. Three months later, there were no signs of her previous reclusiveness.

Erickson's ingenious interventions vitalized the development of strategic therapy, adding creativity and imagination to systems thinking. One of his legacies is the idea that strategies need to be tailor-made to each individual case. Like Tolstoy, Erickson believed that all unhappy families were unhappy in their own way—and therefore the therapist had to create a unique strategy to fit each case.

Since not every therapist can be expected to have the dramatic ingenuity of Milton Erickson, one may ask how the discipline has performed on the therapeutic stage. In fact, a rich body of research, reported in books and journals, has grown up, showing that family therapy is successful with youth violence and drug use, suicidal youth, and young people who are failing at school. Notably, too, family therapy also has a proven record of effectiveness in treating children without medication.

Right from the start, the discipline's methods and results have had a high degree of transparency. In family therapy training centers, sessions are videotaped live (with the faces of the clients blocked out to ensure privacy). A supervisor phones in interventions to the therapist from behind a one-way mirror, with trainees looking on. Trainees thus see exactly what goes on in the sessions. This candid way of revealing which interventions work and which do not is very different from the psychodynamic approach, where the therapist is closeted in the room with a patient, and nobody else witnesses what techniques are used or even whether the therapy is succeeding. In family therapy research studies conducted at major universities, independent raters as well as university supervisors review videotaped sessions, thus ensuring impartial evaluations.

Family therapists are psychologists, social workers, counselors, and even psychiatrists. Some pediatricians—including Lawrence Diller, the California physician who has spoken out against the medicalization of children's misbehavior—also practice family therapy. Family therapy conferences now embrace exciting new research in social neuroscience, and conference speakers include state-of-the-art brain scientists like Daniel Siegel as well as patriarchs of the field like Salvador Minuchin.

Given its innovative approach to human problems—and particularly its proven success in treating children—why has family therapy not been more widely adopted? Probably the most significant reason is that parents, understandably, don't want to feel blamed. Nobody wants their family to be labeled "dysfunctional." Parents have thus felt more comfortable buying into a frame of reference that does not involve them in their child's treatment or in the origins of their child's problems. Also, many parents have busy lives and stressful schedules, which make them prefer to have a health professional "fix" their child without their having to be involved in the therapy themselves.

Do family therapists point the finger at parents, alleging that they are at the root of their children's problems? The answer is a resounding No. In fact, family therapists do not blame parents at all. What we do is help transform patterns of communication and social interaction in the child's family, clarifying boundaries, adjusting alliances, and restoring the family hierarchy. We may ask parents to change certain aspects of parenting, such as being consistent about rules and consequences. We may recommend that parents alter particular aspects of their communication with each other, such as not arguing or yelling in front of their children and making sure to say kind things about the other parent in the children's presence. But making these suggestions for small changes is very different from blaming parents. Central to contemporary family therapy is the belief that the therapist must have a good relationship not only with the child in treatment but with the parents as well. "Joining" the family—which means making each family member feel heard and respected—is one of the oldest and most revered principles of family therapy. Making parents feel blamed would not help children at all.

More than thirty years ago, the child psychoanalyst Dorothy Bloch wrote touchingly about her experience with parents of seriously disturbed children. The parents were in so much pain, Bloch observed, that they could not accept a treatment that involved changing the way they parented their child. In her experience, parents preferred to have their child diagnosed with a serious psychiatric illness like schizophrenia, which they believed to have biological or genetic causes, rather than consider "re-patterning" the way they parent. Parents did not want to admit to themselves that they had anything to do with the origins of their child's problems, and they did not want to participate in treatment, even when Dr. Bloch, a highly respected child psychoanalyst, advised it, and even when it required making changes only in their parenting.

Although she wisely recognized the importance of parents' actions, Dr. Bloch was not a family therapist. She practiced within the tradition of "talk therapy," and this fact points to another reason that psychiatrists, pediatricians, and parents have not paid enough attention to family therapy: they think of it as just another ineffective form of talk therapy. Traditional child therapy is psychodynamic play therapy, with roots in the psychoanalytic "talking cure" tradition. And most pediatricians have learned that individual play therapy is generally ineffective with children. The important exception is in situations where a child has been subjected to a severe trauma such as abuse or molestation. In those cases a supportive therapeutic relationship with an individual therapist, along with play therapy, can help a child heal. But family therapy should always be part of the treatment of a traumatized child. It does not help a child to feel better in the therapist's office only to return to an unsafe or a chaotic family environment where she is re-traumatized day after day. In cases where a child's family is abusive or neglectful, home-based family therapy can help abusive parents become more competent and appropriately caring for their children.

Before I discovered family therapy, I was a play therapist. Like most psychotherapists who worked with children at that time, I furnished my office with a sand tray, shelves of miniature figures, and a variety of toys and games to help children express their conflicts and fears in a safe, supportive setting. Although I often met with the child's parents in an initial session, to get a history of the problem and discover what the parents had tried so far, I never included other family members in my sessions with the children.

One of my earliest patients was an eleven-year-old girl named Mia, who suffered from anxiety and nightmares. She would wake up screaming in the middle of the night and could not express to her parents what was troubling her. In my office, Mia was immediately attracted to the sand tray, and proceeded to mold the damp sand into a huge mound. She patted it and smoothed it carefully and then, with her palm flat, she swept her hand through the mound of sand, leveling it completely. She repeated this action several times, building the mound of sand, and then leveling it with a sweep. As it happened, Mia's mother had been diagnosed with breast cancer and was scheduled for a mastectomy. Mia's sand play thus made sense to me as a visual representation of her fears about her mother. I realized that Mia had probably heard snippets of information about her mother's surgery and was undoubtedly frightened. I thought that this was probably the source of her nightmares.

I talked with Mia's mother privately in the waiting room and suggested that she not discuss her surgery in front of her daughter. I asked her to reassure Mia that she was going to be fine. I also recommended that both parents bring humor and laughter into the family with simple things like reading the comics with Mia in the mornings before school, getting books of jokes and riddles from the library, and watching funny movies. These simple commonsense interventions helped, and after a few more sessions of play therapy, Mia soon stopped having nightmares and anxiety. I think that what helped Mia was not so much the play therapy, where she could express her fears, but what her parents were doing at home to lighten the atmosphere. The play therapy was, if anything, a vehicle for me to intervene with Mia's family.

My experience with Mia triggered a curious realization: the time I spent talking with a child's parents in the waiting room was having more impact on resolving the child's problem than the sessions I spent with the child. Talking with parents in the waiting room, I would make commonsense recommendations like the ones I made to Mia's parents. For a child with behavior problems, I asked the parents not to fight in front of their children and to be consistent about discipline. I suggested that parents pick their battles with their children and never make a threat that they couldn't follow through on. Before long, I came to the conclusion that play therapy, though it was enjoyable for both the child and me, was less effective than what I had started to call "waiting room therapy."

But with some of my more difficult cases, even months of play therapy and conversations with parents produced little or no improvement. So I began to look around for a more effective method of helping children.

This was the early 1990s, when family therapy was in its golden age. At that time, even psychiatry residents at some medical schools were being trained in the discipline, and training institutes were springing up all over the country. Opportunities to study with the leaders of family therapy were abundant in the San Francisco Bay Area, where I lived at that time. Soon I found myself at a workshop with the charismatic master teacher Jay Haley, who showed videotapes and discussed several cases. One of the things that impressed me right away was that the children's presenting problems were solved in an average of seven sessions. *Seven sessions*, I thought to myself. I had sometimes seen a child in play therapy for fifteen sessions with scant improvement. Right there in that workshop, I knew I had found the approach that I was looking for. A few months later, I was on a plane to Washington, D.C.

The Family Therapy Institute, which Jay directed with his wife, Cloe Madanes, was a converted town house in a pleasant neighborhood in Rockville, Maryland. Trainees witnessed live therapy sessions though a one-way mirror, and all sessions were video recorded so that we could review them afterward. What I learned was not merely a new way of doing therapy but also a new way of seeing reality. I no longer *saw* individuals in therapy sessions. I now *saw* only sequences of interactions in families. I saw family members reacting to what other family members said or did. And I saw real change take place— live, in front of my eyes—as if the therapy session was a play and I was sitting in the front row. In one case, when the therapist prodded a passive, disengaged father to raise his voice and tell his sixteen-year-old son to shut up and stop interrupting their conversation, I saw the son instantly metamorphose from a pit bull into a field mouse.

The transformation caused by witnessing such live therapy sessions is an experience that is both profound and immediate. One early family therapist, Augustus Napier, describes his first encounter with master family therapist Carl Whitaker as a "conversion." Napier found this new way of seeing families so exciting that he became a family therapy enthusiast "in a matter of minutes."

In one of my first meetings with Jay, I related my epiphany about the effectiveness of "waiting room therapy." With a chuckle, he gave me one of his papers called "In Defense of Child Therapy"—a thinly veiled satire of traditional child therapy and child therapists. He told me that it was OK to allow a child to play with toys in the room while I met with the child's family, but play therapy by itself would not help. Parents had to be actively involved in the therapy for it to be effective.

For the next few years I had telephone supervision with Jay, calling him long distance from California whenever I had a particularly difficult case. In the early days, I had to have profound trust in Jay as a supervisor to put into action some of the strategies he so confidently suggested. At times, I felt like a skydiver, leaping out of an airplane into thin air with only my confidence in Jay for a parachute. In one case of a nineteen-year-old boy who lived at home and frequently got drunk, I had to ask the boy's parents to pack up all his clothes and remove them from the house, leaving him only a towel to wear so he couldn't go out and buy liquor. The strategy actually worked, with the boy using his towel-clad leisure time at home to teach himself computer skills. He eventually got a good job, moved out, and stopped drinking. What really produced change was for the boy to witness his parents working together as a team instead of hearing them argue all the time. The tactic in so many cases was the same: put the parents in charge of their kid and clarify the boundaries of the parental subsystem. Eventually I became comfortable with asking parents to do some of the off-the-wall things that Jay told me to do because the strategies worked.

Jay always encouraged his students to break away from the known and familiar strategies of the masters and forge our own paths. Because strategic family therapy was in essence a creative endeavor, there were always new challenges for the unique situations that presented themselves to me. By 2003, drawing on my experience with hundreds of children and teenagers and their families in therapy, I had put together my own unique strategic approach, which I called "strategic child-focused family therapy." I began to present my method at family therapy conferences and workshops, in journals, and now in this book.

Although Jay Haley's strategic family therapy was the main fabric of my approach, one other strand of family therapy has had an important influence on my way of thinking. This was the "narrative therapy" of therapists Michael White, in Australia, and David Epston, in New Zealand. Narrative therapists are interested in how society affects the way we characterize people's problems. They believe that psychiatric diagnoses are the prevailing stories or constructions created by groups that hold power in society.

Perceiving diagnoses of conduct disorder, bipolar disorder, attention-deficit disorder, and even anorexia as socially sanctioned stories that can trap young people into being labeled as problems, sometimes for a lifetime, White and Epston searched for new lenses, or what I would call "frames," for classifying the problems that they were seeing in exploding numbers. And they concluded that the most appropriate lenses should come not from the tradition of scientific positivism or biological determinism, which are the dominant narratives for our time, but from the more ancient tradition of stories.

Narrative therapists thus insist that the "problem" is separate from, and external to, the child. This realization gives family therapists, including me, even more zeal to avoid the tricky minefield of childhood psychiatric diagnoses and focus on what actually needs to change in the child's world in order for the child to start feeling better.

Observing the way narrative therapy reframes psychiatric diagnoses not as real illnesses but as socially constructed stories that may dangerously ensnare a child was especially useful in my work with a little boy named Paolo, whom you are now going to meet.

TWO

A New Frame

Strategic Child-Focused Family Therapy

SEVEN-YEAR-OLD PAOLO was a superb student. But two months into the school year, Paolo's second-grade teacher recommended that he be evaluated for ADHD. Alarmed, Paolo's parents called their pediatrician, who referred Paolo to me for an evaluation. Paolo attended a highly rated elementary school in a middle-class suburb that, like many other schools throughout the country, seemed to be experiencing an epidemic of ADHD. His teacher said that Paolo had "focusing" and "attention" difficulties and was disruptive in the classroom. He spoke out of turn and sometimes chatted with his friends instead of working on his class assignments.

I carefully studied the teacher's observations, and then met with Paolo and his parents for two sessions. His parents were intelligent and educated. His father taught economics at a local university, and his mother worked part-time as a pediatric nurse. They both wanted to avoid medication for Paolo. I also spoke with the school counselor, with whom I had often collaborated. Paolo's family had moved to California from the Philippines when Paolo was four, and he still had some trouble expressing himself in English.

Paolo was a sweet boy, with brown hair and liquid brown eyes. In my first session with him, he seemed calm and focused and made good eye contact with me. Apart from his slight difficulty with English, I could find nothing wrong with him. I observed no signs of ADHD or conduct disorder, although he was strong willed and, like most kids his age, liked to get his own way. My consultation with Paolo's parents did not uncover family issues that might be affecting him. At home, they told me, Paolo behaved very well. They rarely had to discipline him. Even so, Paolo's parents decided to attend a parenting class at the local community center. They wanted to do everything they could to help their son.

I reported my observations to the school counselor, who was puzzled that I didn't diagnose Paolo with ADHD. She told me that the school could do many things for a child with ADHD, including receiving resources from the state to pay for an aide in his classroom. But I was still hesitant to diagnose him because I didn't see the symptoms and I didn't want Paolo to be labeled at such a young age with a psychiatric diagnosis that might influence the way his parents and teachers perceived him. I suggested to the school counselor that Paolo sit in the first row of the classroom, since he had told me that he had trouble reading the directions on the blackboard. He also had some problems reading the instructions on the worksheets that the teacher handed out.

Paolo's parents, the school counselor, and I all assumed, incorrectly as it turned out, that Paolo was still having difficulty reading and comprehending English. We all believed that this was the source of his problems. At my suggestion, his parents put him in a private after-school reading program to improve his English comprehension.

His teacher also arranged for him to meet weekly in a small group with the school's reading specialist. We were sure this extra help would resolve the matter. Unfortunately, we were wrong.

After a few weeks, Paolo's teacher sent him back to counseling, this time with a concern that he might be "autistic." She sensed some kind of medical problem, something she couldn't quite put her finger on. I saw Paolo for several more sessions with his parents and could find not a single symptom of ADHD, much less autism—Paolo continued to make good eye contact with me, he talked with me easily, and he was cooperative about putting away toys. His social interactions with his peers seemed normal enough; he had two good friends with whom he had playdates and sleepovers.

By now Paolo was starting to feel terrible about what was happening at school. His self-esteem and self-confidence had started to plummet. With tears streaming down his cheeks, Paolo told me, "I don't want to be a problem anymore." He had lost so much self-confidence that he was afraid to participate in the class play because he feared he wouldn't be able to remember his lines.

The school counselor was pressing me for a diagnosis of ADHD, ODD (oppositional defiant disorder), or even autism. I was surprised at this, but I understood that she had to be sensitive to the teacher's concerns. Paolo wasn't keeping up with his class in reading, and this was a problem for the teacher. Even after his teacher moved him to the first row of the classroom, his work had not improved.

I was stumped. In hopes of buying more time to get to the source of the problem, I told the counselor I thought Paolo was probably having an adjustment issue. On hearing this, Paolo's teacher insisted that his parents consult a psychiatrist or at least a pediatrician to discover the "medical" cause of his problem.

I called Paolo's pediatrician and explained the situation. I told him honestly that I thought that the school was trying to force a diagnosis on this child. Paolo's mother took him in the next day for a thorough physical exam. Even though the pediatrician had checked Paolo eight months earlier, this time he found that the vision in both of his eyes badly needed correction. Paolo wasn't doing his class work because he wasn't able to see.

To be perfectly honest, I should have picked up on Paolo's vision problem myself. One day prior to the pediatrician's diagnosis, Paolo's mother had brought in a math worksheet that she wanted me to work on with Paolo. I read the directions aloud to Paolo, and he worked out the problems perfectly. Then I read him the directions for the next set of problems. Again, he completed them perfectly. I then handed Paolo the directions for the third set of problems, saying that now he could do the worksheet by himself. He handed it back to me, saying, "I like it better when you read the directions to me." So I continued reading him the directions. I should have realized right then and there that he was having trouble seeing the words on the page.

In our last therapy session, a much happier Paolo sported a pair of wire-rimmed metallic gray glasses. Attached to the temples was a red sports band that, he explained to me, kept his glasses from falling off during gym or karate classes. Paolo proudly told me that unlike the days when he could not finish his assignments (because, as it turned out, he could not see the instructions on the blackboard or on the worksheets), now his teacher assigned him extra work like the "smart" kids in his class. He was obviously feeling much better about school and about himself. He finished the school year second in his class.

The wise master therapist Paul Watzlawick once said "words are like bullets." I would rephrase this as "diagnoses are like bullets." An incorrect or hastily made diagnosis can shatter a child's life and reduce the child's family to despair. Yet, in schools all over the country, teachers are diagnosing children with ADHD and other mental disorders.

The worst thing about this trend is, as we saw with Paolo, the child himself starts to identify with the idea that there is something wrong with him. Then he suffers a loss of self-esteem, which turns out to be a problem in itself—thus perpetuating a vicious cycle in which his "problem" becomes a self-fulfilling prophecy.

Paolo's teacher probably would have caught Paolo's vision problem right away if the epidemic of labeling children had not been so pervasive at her school. The teacher was undoubtedly under pressure to have all the children in her classroom meet certain academic milestones. And Paolo was in fact falling behind. The teacher certainly had good intentions. She wanted Paolo, who was very bright, to do his best and succeed to his full potential. Unfortunately, she got so caught up in the frame of psychiatric diagnoses that she did not catch Paolo's vision problem.

Paolo's story is a little different from those of most of the other children in this book because the problem was not with his family. But his story illustrates how the dominant narrative of psychiatric diagnosis can cloud our minds so that we think we know what a child's problem is when actually we are on the wrong track entirely. By not labeling Paolo with a mental health diagnosis, we were able to persist and find the real problem, which could then be easily corrected by a visit to the pediatrician. Of course I learned from this experience. Now, with children who are not doing well at school, I always ask parents if the child has had a recent vision test.

Working within the frame of strategic child-focused family therapy, I approached Paolo's problems without the preconception that he had a mental illness. I first looked for family issues that might be distressing him—such as parental disagreements about discipline, loud arguments, and other stressors at home. After meeting with Paolo's parents over the course of several weeks, and having discussions with the school counselor, who also met with Paolo's parents, we both ruled out family factors. I then formed a tentative hypothesis that Paolo was still having trouble with English comprehension.

In searching for an alternative to a psychiatric diagnosis for Paolo, narrative therapy offered me a powerful framework. Narrative therapists view psychiatric diagnoses as "trends"—such as assigning psychiatric labels to children—that take on a life of their own. These trends become the prevalent ways that people in a particular society ascribe meaning to behaviors, feelings, and events. Narrative therapists encourage therapists to keep an open mind and look beyond the dominant narratives. They suggest that therapists try to discover alternative stories so that therapy can produce "unique outcomes"— such as the outcome of Paolo's story.

In this book I write about children who bring many different problems to therapy. Some of them, like Paolo, have focusing and attention problems and are falling behind in their schoolwork and getting failing grades. Some have anxieties, fears, or compulsive behaviors. Some are aggressive and hostile; they are bullies at school and shunned by their classmates. Some refuse to go to school at all, making excuses that they feel sick. Others are sad to the point of despair. None of these children had been abused or neglected. Their problems were generated in the everyday drama of family life, with its ups and downs, its joys and sorrows, its hopes and disappointments. And the children's problems are resolved in family therapy with the collaboration and cooperation of their parents.

The community where I practice is a middle-class suburb called, picturesquely, the Valley of the Rabbits. Our small valley is tucked in the Santa Monica Mountains about midway between Los Angeles and Santa Barbara. The community abounds with "soccer moms," who pick up their children from school to drive them to parks and playdates, and "hockey dads," who take time off from work to chaperone their children's field trips. It is a child-oriented community with excellent public and private schools. Learning centers and homework clubs thrive, as parents are motivated to give their children the extra help they might need to succeed in school.

Many parents sacrifice vacations and new cars so they can build up college funds for their children. Yet despite all their advantages, these children have problems, sometimes serious ones, and it's my job as a family therapist to help resolve those problems safely, briefly, and effectively, without medication.

My office is on the second floor of a two-story building in a peaceful neighborhood. It is a child-friendly place, filled with sunlight, live plants, and plenty of toys. From my window, there is a view of trees, hills, and sky. The walls are lined with tall oak bookcases containing children's books, puzzles, games, and tiny figurines.

It's in this office that I worked with two children, Laura and Joey, who came to me from different families but shared the most frightful of problems. Joey, four and a half, and Laura, eleven, had both threatened to kill themselves, and Joey had also made a terrifying suicidal gesture. I worked successfully with both children within a family therapy framework. The key to success was looking at the wider social context of the child—to see a boy or girl not merely as an individual but also as part of a larger family system. Laura and Joey came to therapy because they were "hyper"—they were unsettled and irritable, had difficulty falling asleep, and were generally driving their parents crazy. Both of their mothers had been diagnosed with bipolar disorder and had been taking psychiatric medications for many years. Each mother was afraid that her child, like herself, might have bipolar disorder. In both cases, the child's teachers had recommended psychiatric evaluation.

Weighing just sixty-two pounds, Laura was a tiny slip of a girl, with short curly black hair and piercing dark eyes that seemed huge in her thin face. When I met her I thought she was nine or maybe ten, although she was just past her eleventh birthday. Laura had been taking psychiatric medications since second grade, when her mother consulted a child psychiatrist because Laura "couldn't sit still" and focus in the classroom. Now Laura was taking eight pills a day for ADHD, depression, and anxiety. She had little appetite, which her psychiatrist said was a side effect of the Adderall that she took for ADHD. Laura's pediatrician was concerned that she was "severely underweight."

In spite of the medications, Laura still had trouble falling asleep and had periods of lethargy and depression. She was failing several subjects because she wasn't turning in her homework assignments. Terrified when Laura said, "I want to kill myself," Laura's mother, Elise, brought her to therapy.

Elise, a single parent who worked as a project manager for a medical device company, had raised her daughter mainly by herself. She was a tall, attractive woman in her early forties with intense brown eyes. The day we met, her curly black hair was tucked under a navy blue Texas Rangers baseball cap. She had grown up in Texas and spoke with a soft southern drawl. Something about Elise's intensity reminded me of a lioness fiercely protecting her cub. She seemed determined to get to the root of her daughter's problem no matter what it took. At the same time, the tomboyish way she dressed and the baseball cap she always wore to our therapy sessions gave a faint suggestion of masculinity.

Elise told me that Laura's biological father, Jeff, had died tragically in a motorcycle accident when Laura was two. Elise's parents had disapproved of her marrying Jeff because he was not a member of their church, but after Jeff died the grandparents had become more involved with their daughter and only granddaughter. For the past six years, Elise had been living with Jim, whom she met at Parents without Partners. Laura called Jim "Daddy." Jim was a good friend and companion to Elise and a fine father figure to Laura.

While Elise was telling me their story, Laura sat quietly on the couch very close to her mother. She seemed strangely subdued and unchildlike, showing little interest in the shelves of toys and games.

Instead of doing a puzzle or looking at a book, Laura listened attentively to every word her mother said to me.

Elise told me she had been diagnosed with bipolar disorder nine
years ago, around the time of her husband's death, and was currently
taking three psychiatric medications. I could see that Elise loved her
daughter very much. She had struggled to raise her by herself without her husband until her parents decided to help her. Elise now had
a good job and could afford to send Laura to an excellent private
school. Jim was a teacher at a nearby high school, so it was easy for
him to pick up Laura from school and bring her home every day.

Seeing the love between mother and daughter and the mother's
obvious kindness and warmth toward her daughter, I hypothesized
that Laura's problems had to do with attempting to help her mother
in some way. It was as though she were trying to pick up her mother's
burdens and carry them on her own thin shoulders. And no matter
how depressed Elise might get, she had to pull herself together in
order to take care of her daughter and drive her to appointments.

I, like most family therapists, find it useful to think of a child's
problem or symptom as having a benevolent purpose in the family. I
assume that a child's problem is in some way helpful to or protective
of a parent. It also made sense to me that Laura would have a school-
related problem because Elise valued education so highly. But Laura's
problem might also indicate that her mother was having a problem
at work—because, as we will see, a child's problem often mirrors a
parent's problem. I would keep this hypothesis in mind when I spoke
privately with Elise.

As I always do when I believe that a child is helping a parent by
having a symptom, I told Laura casually but pointedly, "I will be
the helper now," gesturing toward her mother when I said the word .
"helper." I was suggesting to Laura that I would take the burden of
benevolence off her shoulders. I was implicitly asking her to trust me
to help her mother so that she would not have to. Laura nodded to

show that she had understood what I was saying. Then I asked Laura to pick out some books and puzzles and take them to the waiting room while I "helped" her mother. I assured Laura that she could come back into the office anytime she wanted. Laura agreed eagerly, picked up a set of colored pencils and paper from the shelf, and left the room.

The first thing I did when Elise and I were alone was to ask if she talked about her own problems in front of her daughter. "Yes," she replied, "I don't hide anything from her."

"I would like to ask you to change that," I said, "and in fact I want you to tell Laura every day what a good day you had at work. I would like you to tell her every morning that you are looking forward to your day (you make up the reason why) and tell her every evening why you enjoyed your day. You'll have to arrange lunches with friends, workouts at the gym, or whatever, so you'll be telling her the truth."

Elise seemed surprised at this suggestion, but she readily agreed, saying, "I'll do this if you think it will help."

"I know it will," I replied, hoping to bolster Elise's confidence in her ability to help her daughter.

The Greek mathematician and engineer Archimedes is reputed to have said, "Give me a place to stand on and with a lever I will move the whole earth." He was describing the powerful principle of leverage. Although the lever is a simple device, it can move weighty things. Similarly, the simple strategic move of asking a mother to talk only about positive things in her life is a powerful lever, and it's one of the most important tools in my strategic therapy toolbox. This strategy reassures a child that her mother is fine and does not need the child to help her.

Then I continued. "Don't let Laura overhear you telling Jim or any of your friends about your problems at work. Assume that Laura will hear everything you say, even when you're in your room upstairs talking quietly on the phone. Try to let her overhear only positive things. If you have an argument with Jim, as couples do, don't let Laura hear about it." I explained to Elise that Laura was very protective of her mother and felt that her mother was unhappy. Elise said she was willing to try anything to help her daughter, and agreed to do as I said.

Over the next few weeks, I spent the first minutes of each session listening to Laura's concerns. At first she said she was worried that her mother's job was too stressful. She thought her mother hated her boss because he had not given her a promotion last year. She said her mother was always tired when she came home from work. I spent the remainder of the sessions "helping" her mother while Laura did her homework in the waiting room.

Elise was a quick study. In one session, when I asked her "How was your day?" in front of Laura, Elise told me convincingly that she had had "a very good day." She had gone out for lunch with a co-worker to a great new restaurant. I could tell that Elise was following my instructions at home. Laura's grades improved steadily until her semester grades were all B's except for a B– in science. We then worked on strategies to help Laura eat more. Elise began keeping frozen lasagnas and pizzas in the freezer, so Jim could make Laura a hearty snack and a milk shake after school. I asked Laura to discuss with her mother the kinds of foods she preferred to eat. She immediately said that she liked strawberries and bananas in her milk shakes, and vegetarian pizzas. They made a shopping list together right in the session.

The first week, Laura gained a pound, and in the following weeks her weight continued to climb steadily. There were a few backslides, and once we had to intervene with one of Laura's teachers; a boy who sat next to Laura was making annoying comments to her, so the teacher had Laura move to the front of the classroom. After nine sessions of therapy over the course of five and a half months, Laura was down to a single dose of ADHD medication, which she took in the morning before school. Elise told me that Laura would continue the medication until school ended in mid-June and would stop taking it during the summer. Laura's psychiatrist had agreed to wean her from the drugs. Laura was eating much better and had gained four pounds.

The change in Laura's appearance was dramatic. She no longer looked wan and thin. She was more animated, and her black eyes were bright. She looked less like the subdued zombie who had first walked into my office and more like a lively, healthy child. When Elise expressed concern that Laura was too "bouncy" to sit still and do her homework and class work, I reassured her: "She's a child. 'Bouncy' is fine. She is behaving appropriately for her age. If you or Jim sit with her while she does her homework, she will be able to focus better." I also suggested that Laura have some time to play outdoors before she started her homework. Elise said she felt so relieved that her daughter was no longer taking eight pills a day and seemed much happier that she could live with the "bouncy" girl her daughter had become. She assured me that she or Jim would sit at the kitchen table with Laura while she did her homework and help her stay on task.

Strategically reframing a child's problem as helpfulness rather than a psychiatric symptom, and communicating to the child that the therapist is ready to take on the role of the parent's "helper," are powerful instruments of change. Both of these interventions aim at producing change in the larger system of which the child is a part. Looking at the system rather than the individual is what gives the family therapist the leverage she needs to produce quick, effective change. This is the concept that early family therapists learned from systems theory. In all sorts of social systems, small changes can have wide-reaching effects.

...   .

In working with four-and-a-half-year-old Joey, I used the same two strategies I used with Laura—reframing the child's problem as helpful and having a parent say only positive things about her life in front of the child—plus one other simple intervention to get him to stop worrying about his parents and to stop misbehaving.

Joey's parents brought him to family therapy on the advice of their pediatrician, who told them that in his opinion "a four-year-old child was too young to diagnose and medicate." Rather than labeling Joey with a psychiatric diagnosis, he told the parents to "go work on your own issues." The pediatrician was framing Joey's problems as rooted in his family context rather than in his biological makeup.

Joey had been a difficult baby and had had behavior problems since he was two years old. He was defiant and explosive, and lately he had started to scratch and bite his parents and sometimes bang his head against the floor. Getting Joey to bed at night was a "nightmare." He repeatedly came out of his room and asked for a glass of water or a snack, or to be taken to the bathroom. His parents were worn out. Sometimes Joey's explosive episodes were so severe that his parents had to use physical restraint to keep him in time-outs. (Their pediatrician had advised them to restrain Joey if necessary.) When Joey started having violent outbursts at preschool, his teacher recommended medical evaluation. Then one day Joey grabbed a sharp knife and threatened to kill his parents and himself. His mother was horrified and called me to make an appointment.

The first session, early one morning in autumn, was with Joey's parents, Amanda and Richard Whitefield, a couple in their early thirties. They had recently relocated to California from Virginia. Amanda had shoulder-length brown hair, brown eyes, and olive skin. She worked as a receptionist in a small law firm. Dressed for work, since she would be going there directly from our appointment, she wore a powder blue pantsuit and a pearl necklace with matching earrings. Richard, tall, lanky, and dressed in a plaid flannel shirt and khaki trousers, struck me as particularly intelligent and perceptive. He was an engineer at an aerospace company.

The couple confessed that they had second thoughts about the wisdom of having moved to California. Richard's job was more stressful than they had imagined it would be, and it required frequent travel. And now Amanda had to work full-time because of the high cost of living in Los Angeles. In Virginia, Amanda had been able to stay home to take care of Joey and his younger brother, Alan.

When I asked Richard and Amanda how they disciplined Joey, they acknowledged that most of the time they were not on the same page. While Amanda was patient and consistent, Richard started out being calm but soon lost his cool and usually ended up yelling at Joey. They admitted they fought in front of Joey. Richard's job was stressful, and sometimes when he came home from work he would vent at Amanda. Amanda was resentful that they had relocated for Richard's job; she missed her family and friends back in Virginia. Life had been much easier for her there, with her mother always willing to babysit, and her sister—whose children were about the same age as Joey and Alan—available for outings and visits. The couple told me that they were having more marital problems lately. They disagreed about how clean the house was kept and about how to spend their time on weekends. They argued about money; Richard was angry with Amanda because he thought she spent too much. The tension between them was almost palpable when the topic of money came up.

One of the first things I learned as a family therapist was that if a child is violently angry, he might be deflecting one parent's anger from the other parent, "taking the bullet," so to speak. At the same time, a child may also be acting out the anger in his parents' marriage. If there is unexpressed anger in a family, any member of that family can feel or act out the anger because a family is an organic unity, something like a human body. A problem in one part of the body—say a pinched nerve in the neck—can manifest itself as pain or numbness in another part of the body, like an arm or a shoulder. Similarly, a feeling in one area of a family system—say, anger between parents—can manifest itself somewhere else, usually in a child. A family therapist sees a family not merely as a collection of people but as a living organism.

When I met Joey, in the second family session, I became convinced that the anger between his parents was indeed at the root of his behavior problems. Joey was an adorable little boy, with his mother's dark hair and his father's tall, lanky build. He wore blue jeans and a blue T-shirt with "Dodgers" written across it in white script. At first he was fidgety and didn't want to make eye contact with me. Like Laura, he sat very close to his mother on the couch. As I talked with his parents, Joey began to relax. At my invitation, he got up, chose some Lego blocks from a huge yellow barrel in the play area of my office, and began building an airplane.

Toward the end of the session, I spoke with Joey alone for a few minutes while his parents read magazines in the waiting room. First Joey told me that "Daddy doesn't like his job." When I asked how he knew that, he said that his father yelled at his mother when he came home from work in the evening. He added, "Sometimes Daddy yells at me when he gets home." I could see that what Joey was doing by misbehaving was to make his father angry with him, so that his father would yell at him instead of his mother. By drawing his father's fire, Joey was protecting his mother. The goals of therapy, then, would be to help Richard with his stress and anger. I would also have to help him become more patient with Joey, so that the parents would be more calm and consistent about discipline. I used a few of my usual strategies to accomplish these goals.

First, I asked Amanda and Richard to tell Joey every morning that they were looking forward to their day, and in the evening they would tell Joey one enjoyable thing they had done that day. I asked Richard to say something nice to Amanda every day when he came home, to occasionally bring her a small gift such as flowers, and not to argue with her in front of Joey. I asked both parents not to raise their voices in Joey's presence. I also recommended that Richard take ten minutes to reflect on his day before coming into the house after work. This would give him some "cooling off" time if he had had a bad day. Richard admitted that his job was disappointing; it was not what he had been expecting when he signed on with the company. He felt that his real skills were not being used, and this was frustrating to him. He was aware that this distress was affecting his mood at home. Amanda listened attentively to Richard. "He doesn't usually talk about work," she said with sympathy in her voice.

Then I gave the parents a simple paradoxical strategy to use with Joey at bedtime. They were to put Joey to bed, and every five minutes one of them was to go into his room and ask him if he wanted to get a drink of water or a snack, go to the bathroom, get a book—all the excuses Joey used for not going to bed. For fifteen minutes Amanda was to supervise Joey's "not going to bed." Here, I was paradoxically prescribing the very behavior that we wanted to change, trusting that Joey would rebel against his mother taking control of his bedtime antics. The idea is that telling a child to have a problem behavior takes away its spontaneity. It makes the problem into a chore, something that he must do instead of something that gets his parents' attention. Paradoxical strategies are at the very heart of family therapy; I say more about them in Chapter 6.

Amanda started the third therapy session by reporting a "huge improvement" in Joey's behavior. There had been no incidents of angry defiance either at home or at preschool. Joey's parents were being more positive around him, and Richard wasn't yelling when he came home after work. He was taking a few minutes to listen to music in his car and think about his day before coming into the house. He also had started jogging in the morning before work, and he said it helped him feel less stressed.

Now that the parents had seen the effects of therapy in their child, they became more open about their own relationship. Amanda and Richard had the usual laundry list of little annoyances that, if not attended to, mount up over time into a great wall of resentment. Little by little, we discussed the small behaviors that each one could change. Amanda agreed to put away her shoes and jacket instead of leaving them wherever she happened to drop them. Richard agreed to remember to walk their dog in the mornings before work. I also recommended that the couple find a babysitter and go out on a date by themselves. They hadn't gone out alone for more than six months.

Richard was able to make a few changes at work that helped to relieve his stress. After three months, with biweekly marriage counseling and focused parenting advice, Joey had no more violent outbursts and no longer banged his head against the floor. He was also more cooperative about going to bed at night. I had recommended that Joey get involved in sports as an outlet for his high energy. Richard was taking him to the park on Saturdays to practice softball, and they planned to sign up Joey for soccer in the summer.

I had reframed Joey's violence and misbehavior as benevolent to both of his parents. By acting out when his father came home from work, Joey had made his father angry with him, thus sparing his mother his father's harsh words. Joey's misbehavior had also distracted his parents from their own troubles: their marital difficulties, financial problems, social isolation, and the distress that his father was suffering at work. Joey's problem behaviors had the salutary effect of uniting his parents to work together to resolve their son's problems by having to meet with his teacher, his pediatrician, and ultimately with me for marital therapy.

When Joey saw that his parents were no longer arguing with each other and his father was less stressed when he came home from work, he could give up his misbehaviors because they had finished serving their purpose. Joey made no further threats or gestures of suicide.

A child will usually give up his problem behaviors when he trusts the therapist to take over his role of helping and protecting his parents. For Laura and Joey, direct strategies were sufficient to achieve the goals of therapy because the parents were willing and also able to follow my directions. I used only one indirect strategy, in asking Joey's mother to supervise him "not going to bed." In a more difficult case that I present later on, a child's parents were not able to follow my directions even though they wanted to. I explain how I used an indirect strategy with these parents, getting them to rebel against my directions.

Choosing to frame a child's disruptive and violent behaviors as helpful to his parents instead of as signs of a "mental illness"—which may exist one day and disappear the next—is a simple reframing of events. But the act of reframing can have powerful effects, and reframing is one of the family therapist's most important tools.

To see how useful a small strategic intervention can be, consider a charming case of reframing with which most readers are familiar. When rascally Tom Sawyer wanted to get his friend Ben to take over the chore of whitewashing his Aunt Polly's fence, Tom simply reframed the task as a coveted privilege rather than work. Nothing changed about the act of whitewashing. What changed was Ben's way of thinking about it. Tom Sawyer was thinking like a strategic family therapist.

Family therapists frame children's problems as responses to family situations and life transitions, such as illness, job problems, or marital difficulties. Sometimes a child may also struggle with a developmental hurdle such as learning to talk or mastering reading. In this situation, the therapist focuses on the specific hurdle rather than diagnosing the child's problem as one symptom in a cluster that together constitute a psychiatric disorder.

Not long ago a pediatrician in a nearby town offered me one of the most striking and useful reframes in my experience as a family therapist. His reframing of one child's problem made all the difference in the world to his little patient. The pediatrician, whom I will call Dr. R., referred two-and-a-half-year-old Briana to family therapy for severe behavior problems and a speech problem.

At our first session, Briana swept into my office like a blond whirlwind. In minutes, she reduced the playroom to a chaotic jumble of blocks, puzzles, books, and toys. When I tried to talk to her, she wouldn't look at me. As she relentlessly pulled one object after another off the shelves, Briana sang to herself in an unintelligible babble. She blithely ignored her mother's pleas to put some of the toys back on the shelf before taking another one. When her mother offered her a wooden puzzle with pictures of jungle animals, Briana simply turned it upside down, scattering the pieces all over the floor. Seizing a box of crayons, she started to scribble on a page of *Curious George*. At that point I intervened and asked her to stop.

Briana's parents, Joan and Martin Lopez, were in their late thirties. Joan had frizzy honey blond hair and blue eyes. Martin, dark haired and dark eyed, had a goatee that made him look distinguished. They had moved to Los Angeles from Argentina a little more than a year ago. Joan told me that they were at their wit's end about what to do with their unruly daughter. At the end of every day, they were totally exhausted. Briana demanded so much of her parents' attention that they were always too tired to help their two older children with their homework. They never seemed to have time to spend with each other. Fortunately, their babysitter, a teenager who lived in their neighborhood, prepared simple dinners for the family before leaving at 5:30. "If it weren't for the babysitter, none of us would have dinner," said Joan. At bedtime, Briana screamed and sobbed and refused to go to sleep until her mother lay down next to her. Whenever Briana woke up in the middle of the night, she came into her parents' bed. They didn't have the energy to take her back to her room, so she slept with them the rest of the night.

After my first appointment with Briana and her parents, I called Dr. R. to ask him if he was worried about Briana's having symptoms of autism. I was concerned that she wouldn't look at me directly and didn't talk at the typical level for her age. The pediatrician warned me, in a worried tone: "Don't use the word 'autism' when you treat Briana, because both of her parents are doctors. Treat her for behavior problems and a speech delay." I couldn't have been more pleased to hear these words, as that was exactly what I had been planning to do.

Dr. R. was from Europe, where medical diagnosis of children's behavioral problems is far less common than in the United States; and he understood the importance of framing this child's problems in nonmedical terms. Neither he nor I ever diagnosed Briana with autism or autistic spectrum disorder, although her chaotic angry behavior, unwillingness to make eye contact, unintelligible babble, speech delay, and general unhappiness might well have landed her with a psychiatric diagnosis in the eyes of other health professionals.

I recommended to Briana's parents that they come in alone to tell me their family's story. I met with them the following week. The most striking thing about this couple's relationship was the imbalance of power in their marriage. Martin, originally from Argentina, had given up a brilliant career as a surgeon to move to the United States. He and Joan had met and married in Buenos Aires, where Martin was a surgery resident and Joan was in medical school. After Briana was born, Joan wanted to return to California, where her parents and sisters lived. Her mother had just been diagnosed with cancer, and Joan wanted to live closer to her. But Martin had been reluctant to leave his career and his family in Argentina. Eventually, Joan persuaded him to move, arguing that their children would have more opportunities in the United States and that her mother needed her.

Joan found a research position at a university in Los Angeles. Martin had to spend his days studying for a series of medical board exams in order to apply for a surgery residency in this country. He told me that he felt very frustrated. In Buenos Aires he had been a respected surgeon. In this country he had to start all over again with board exams and a whole new residency. The exams were even more of a challenge because his English was less than perfect. Martin missed his parents and his two brothers, with whom he had always been close. He confessed that he had been feeling miserable ever since they had moved to California.

While her husband poured out the torrent of pain that had been building up in him for over a year, Joan listened attentively. When Martin finished speaking, Joan asked him what she could do to make him feel better. Martin said that he would like to visit his parents more often. He also said that if he did not pass the board exams and secure a surgery residency in this country, he wanted their family to move back to Argentina. With some reluctance, Joan agreed to this. She saw how miserable her husband was without his career, and she saw that his unhappiness was affecting their marriage and their daughter.

While they were still living in Argentina, Martin and Joan had consulted a child psychiatrist about their older daughter's behavior problems at school. The psychiatrist helped them see that their daughter's misbehavior expressed the conflicts that the couple was having at home. Although they had changed their behavior, and their older daughter had improved, now they were falling back into the same old patterns. They knew they weren't spending enough time alone together to nurture their marriage. They argued about money and whether moving had been the right decision. When their children finally went to sleep every night, they were too tired to spend quality time together.

I recommended that the couple try to go out to lunch or dinner once a week. They should discuss whatever disagreements they might have in private, away from their home and children. I asked them not to argue at all in front of their children. One major issue with this couple was their different attitudes toward time. Martin believed in being punctual and Joan was always late. After agreeing on what time they would leave for an outing, Martin ended up waiting in the car with Briana and their older daughter while Joan took her time getting dressed or putting on her makeup. This made Martin feel disrespected and angry. Briana, experiencing the tension between her parents, usually started to scream.

Joan was furious that Martin called his mother in Argentina every other night. In her opinion, these expensive phone calls took too much time away from their family. I suggested a trade-off: Joan would be careful to be punctual and not keep Martin waiting, and Martin would spend less time on the phone with his mother. This arrangement seemed to work, and eventually there was less tension between them.

Joan and Martin were responsive to my other suggestions as well. Thanks to what the psychiatrist in Argentina had told them, they were able to recognize that their marital strife was affecting their younger child. I continued to see the couple in marriage counseling, and they brought Briana in occasionally for a family session in which we focused on being consistent about rules and not giving in to Briana's tantrums. Her mother encouraged Briana to use words rather than scream when she wanted a toy she couldn't reach. Briana also had weekly sessions with a speech therapist. Speech problems can be very frustrating to children, fueling their misbehavior and also causing problems when other children sometimes make fun of their mispronunciations.

After Briana spent five months in speech therapy, her speech and conduct had improved enormously. She now spoke to me in simple sentences. Her play became less chaotic. Rather than throwing toys around the floor, she would focus on a simple puzzle and complete it by herself or ask her mother to help her. She would bring a toy or blocks over to her mother and ask her to play. We were careful to praise her and smile every time she used words to name something or ask for a toy.

Most striking was Briana's increasingly affectionate relationship with her mother. She made eye contact with Joan and listened to what her mother said to her. Joan told me that she was spending more quality time with Briana after work and on weekends. "Taking her to the park is fun now because she doesn't just throw the sand around like she used to do," Joan remarked. "Now she plays in the sand with the other children."

Briana even gave me a kiss on the cheek one day when she said good-bye. "Go park now," Briana told me happily at the end of one session, taking her mother by the hand.

As her parents improved their relationship and the tension at home ebbed, they were able to take charge of Briana more effectively. Briana's tantrums and demands for attention decreased. Most important, she seemed much happier. Because the pediatrician intervened early with Briana and because he was able to step outside the dominant narrative of mainstream pediatrics to frame her problems, he saved her from ever having a psychiatric diagnosis.

Can any child with symptoms as severe as Briana's improve as dramatically as she did? Not necessarily. Family therapy is an art, not a science. We cannot generalize or predict results with absolute certainty. But five decades of research have revealed factors that give a child like Briana the best chance of being helped. We know that a child's behavior improves when her parents improve their relationship, when they stop fighting in front of the child, and when they are consistent and back up each other on discipline.

Also contributing to success is that all the health professionals involved with the child were on the same page regarding treatment. Dr. R. and I agreed to frame Briana's problems as developmental issues and not as symptoms of a psychiatric disorder. Most important, Briana's parents were willing to trust a family therapist and give my recommendations a sincere try. They were willing to accept a role in their daughter's treatment without blaming themselves or feeling blamed by me.

As a family therapist, I chose to see Briana's silence as an expression of her father's unvoiced pain and frustration. I sought the source of her father's unhappiness in order to make changes in the family dynamics that would help him—and ultimately help his daughter. I don't expect everyone to see Briana's symptoms this way, and I don't claim that my point of view is a factual truth. As Jay Haley once said, family therapists make up a story about why a child is having a symptom. Then we see if our story is helpful. As it turned out, my story about the source of Briana's problem provided a valuable way to help her as well as her parents.

The same is true of the notion of protectiveness that was so valuable in treating Joey and Laura. My hypothesis or story that a child's problem has a protective function in the family system allows me to help the child and solve the problem. In the next chapter, we will learn more about how a child's problem behaviors can be protective of a parent.

THREE

Listening to Children

WE ALL KNOW THE PROVERB "little pitchers have big ears," which means, of course, that children hear and understand much more of adult conversations than we realize. Children—even young children—are especially prone to eavesdropping on conversations between parents on important matters such as a parent's health or his job. This is precisely what happened with Alex, an adorable five-year-old boy with curly blond hair and blue eyes.

"I'm worried about Daddy because he doesn't have an occupation," Alex said to me. What in the world does he mean by that? I wondered. Alex and I were sitting on the pale blue carpet in my office playing a game of Don't Break the Ice. *Occupation,* I mused. What an unusual word for a five-year-old. I asked Alex what he meant, and he replied, "Daddy doesn't go to work anymore because he doesn't have an occupation." Then he added in a small voice, "We don't have any money to buy new toys or go on trips."

Now I understood. Alex was worried because his father was out of work. I would have to pursue that topic with his parents. I wondered how Alex's mother and father were handling his unemployment. Perhaps they had been talking or arguing about his father not having an occupation, and Alex had overheard them. Or maybe he had heard the word at school. Someone might have asked him what his father's occupation was.

In my practice, children are my scouts and my co-therapists. They lead me across unfamiliar terrain right to the heart of their family's problems, which is an all-too-familiar landscape to them. I had just asked Alex my usual question, "Are you more worried about your mommy or your daddy?" and he had told me. Then I had reassured him that now I was going to be his family's helper, and the worrying would be up to me. I told him that I would meet with his parents alone. "Is that okay with you?" I asked him. Alex nodded his head.

I don't know if it's the kind way in which I ask the question, or whether children simply feel relieved when I say that I am going to help their parents, but I have found that most children respond positively. If a child is at all hesitant to tell me who he is more worried about, I rephrase the question. I say, a little playfully, "Just *pretend* that you are worried about one of your parents. Which one would it be?" or "*If* you were worried about one parent, would it be Mommy or Daddy?" Moving into the realm of make-believe usually prompts even the shyest child to answer. I have never had a child refuse to answer because he is worried about getting into trouble. Children seem to instinctively trust that I am asking only so I can help their family.

We finished our game. Alex won.

When Alex's parents, Jackie and Logan Harrison, had brought him to therapy that morning, the first thing I noticed was the large cast on Logan's right arm. I didn't make much of it until after my conversation with Alex, which took place later in the session.

"Alex has always been a little hyper," Logan said when I asked the couple what had brought them to therapy. "But now it's gotten to the point where we get a call from his kindergarten teacher every day about him kicking or biting other children. He never did that before. His teacher says that he doesn't follow directions in class and won't sit still. He keeps jumping out of his chair and roaming around the room. And he doesn't listen when the teacher talks to him. He runs ahead when the class is going to the playground. Once he almost ran into the street."

"We had a meeting with his teacher last week," Jackie added. "She thinks he might have ADHD. So we took him to the pediatrician, and he said that Alex was 'just behaving like a typical boy.' But when we told him that Alex was about to be kicked out of kindergarten, he recommended we see you. He thought family therapy might really be helpful."

"Alex did seem to have more tantrums after the baby was born," Jackie said. She went on to explain. "We have another son, Andy. He's six months old."

This isn't unusual, I thought. Many children react to the birth of a sibling with some sort of acting out because they feel displaced or dethroned. Some regression is predictable. Sometimes the older child even wants to drink from a bottle or has "accidents" and needs to wear a diaper at night. Did Alex's parents give him enough special attention after the baby came home? I wondered.

As though she were reading my thoughts, Jackie said, "My parents came to stay with us for a month to help us right after Andy was born, so Logan and I spent lots of extra time with Alex while they babysat. We took him to special places, like the circus and the beach. He never had tantrums while we were out with him."

"And now is Alex misbehaving at home also, or is it just at school?" I asked.

"He doesn't want to do anything we ask him to do at home, and he doesn't calm down easily. Putting him to bed takes a long time," Logan said.

While her husband was talking, Jackie looked overwhelmed and about to cry.

In their early thirties, Jackie and Logan were an attractive couple, but they seemed preoccupied and tense. When I asked Logan about the cast, he told me he had broken his arm when he fell on the tennis court four weeks ago. The arm was almost healed enough for the cast to come off. "And I can't wait," he said.

"It's been a really hard time for him," Jackie said with concern in her voice. "And for us." The tears were flowing now. "Logan is usually so active. And he misses his work terribly."

Meanwhile, Alex was playing quietly with a set of trains, making me wonder what was going on to cause so much "hyperactivity." I asked Jackie and Logan about their family. "We have just the two boys, Alex and Andy," said Jackie, smiling now. "Andy is with the babysitter this morning, but she's only part-time." Her voice trailed off.

"Alex adores his baby brother," Logan assured me.

Jackie nodded in agreement and then added, "But of course we wonder if he might sometimes feel jealous."

"We tried to make Alex feel especially loved after Andy was born, but Jackie needed more time to take care of Andy," said Logan. He added, almost apologetically, "Our kindergarten only goes till one in the afternoon, so we put Alex in an after-school program three days a week. He was doing fine there, until recently."

Then, Logan told me, he broke his arm and had to go on disability leave. He was a tennis coach and couldn't do his job with his arm in a cast. Logan was concerned that his time off from work put a financial strain on the family. His disability checks helped, but they didn't cover everything. He also used to earn quite a bit of extra income from taking on private students after work, and of course that income was gone now. And they both agreed that Jackie shouldn't go back to work yet because the baby needed her. She was now on maternity leave with half-pay.

At this point I had asked if the parents would step out to the waiting room so I could speak with Alex privately. That's when the boy told me what was on his mind—that his father didn't have an "occupation." Inviting his parents back into my office, with Alex playing quietly on the floor, I asked them when the teacher had started sending home notes about Alex's behavior. They said it was about six weeks ago.

"So it started around the time that Logan broke his arm?" I asked. They thought about this, and then Logan replied with surprise in his voice that yes, it was right around that time.

"Do you think my accident had something to do with Alex's misbehavior?" he asked incredulously.

"Possibly," I answered. I suggested that Logan and Jackie come back the next day to talk with me. I wanted to speak with them alone and give them some strategies to help Alex. Then I looked at Alex and said with a smile, "Remember, I'm the helper now." We exchanged high fives.

In the session with Alex's parents, I shared with them what Alex had told me: he was worried about his father's not having an "occupation." Logan and Jackie laughed at the word, but they were surprised, even shocked, that their son was so aware of his father's health issues and his work situation. They weren't sure where Alex had heard that word. "Maybe at school," I suggested. Then Jackie remembered that she and Logan had been arguing, and she had said something like "It's all because of your occupation that you broke your arm."

"Could Alex have overheard you?" I asked.

"Sure," said Logan. "He was in the room." But Logan could scarcely believe that his injury was troubling his son so much and causing him to behave badly. He just did not see the connection. "Is that usual for a child his age?" he asked me.

I explained to Logan that it is typical for a child to notice these things and have worrisome fantasies about what they mean. Did he believe that his father would never go back to work because he no longer had a job? Did he think the cast would stay on forever or his mother would always be sad? Young children have a tenuous grasp on the future, and fears like this are not uncommon. We couldn't know exactly what was on Alex's mind, but we needed to get him to stop worrying. It was that simple. To accomplish this, I asked Logan to reassure Alex every day that he still had a job and would be going back to work very soon. I even suggested that Logan take Alex to the tennis club where he coached, so Alex could see for himself what his father's "occupation" was like.

"Have you ever taken him to work with you?" I asked Logan.

"No," he said. "But there is no reason why I couldn't take him there and show him around. That's a good idea."

I asked both parents to reassure Alex that his father's arm was healing and he would soon be back to his normal routine. It was the most important strategy for this family. I also asked them not to discuss financial matters in front of Alex, and to say upbeat things about their lives when Alex was around. Even when a parent is unemployed, he can still tell a child some positive things such as, "I went hiking today with an old friend and it was fun." They agreed to focus on the positive around Alex.

Then, as I typically recommend with very active kids, I suggested that they enroll Alex in a sport like soccer or T-ball, so he would be tired out by bedtime. Another strategy was for his parents to make a star chart to reward his good behavior. For every day that Alex got ready for school on time and went to bed without fussing, he would get a gold star. If he had a good day at school and his teacher did not call his parents or send a note home, he would get an additional star. At the end of the week, eight out of a possible ten gold stars would earn him a trip to the ice-cream shop with one of his parents.

The Harrisons were very health conscious and rarely ate ice cream or other sweets. So this would be a special treat. Also, it would give Alex time alone with one parent without his baby brother. Jackie and Logan liked the idea of a star chart and agreed to try it for two weeks.

At the next session two weeks later, they told me happily that Alex had had "a great two weeks!" They were using the star chart and rewarding Alex with trips to his favorite ice-cream store. Logan reassured Alex every day about his health and his job. He told him that his arm was healing very quickly and he would soon be back at work. He had taken Alex to the tennis club twice and introduced him to the other coaches and some of his students. Alex's behavior at school had improved. At a parent-teacher conference, the teacher was surprised he wasn't on meds for his "ADHD." She was amazed at so much improvement in such a short time.

Because there was a dramatic change in Alex's behavior, I could tell that the parents were following my recommendations consistently. Seeing this kind of rapid improvement is not unusual in family therapy. Once Alex told me which parent he was worried about, I could immediately start to make changes in the family dynamics. If Alex had gone to a play therapist, he might have eventually expressed in play his fears that his father was injured and might never go back to work. This would certainly have made Alex feel better at the time, but his behavior probably would not have improved until his father's arm had actually healed and Alex saw with his own eyes that Logan indeed had an "occupation."

Jackie and Logan said they wanted to follow up in a month. At that meeting, they said there had been no more incidents at school, and bedtime was much less difficult. Alex had started playing T-ball and came home exhausted after practices and games. He now fell asleep at night with few problems. Logan's arm had finished healing and he was finally back at work.

Stories are a way we make sense of our experience. Where the story starts and what is included in it depend on the goals of the storyteller. When Alex's parents told me he might have ADHD, my goal was to find an alternative story to this medical diagnosis. I asked myself, "What was this little boy worried about and when did his worrying begin? What else could be part of the story of his misbehavior?" And, as it happened, Alex's school problems coincided in time with his father's injury. Alex had been an active child before that, but his behavior had not been a problem at school. Creating this story—that Alex was upset about his father's injury—allowed me to remove the worry from his shoulders. I also considered his new brother as a possible cause of Alex's problems. But the timing wasn't right. Yes, Alex had tantrums around the time his brother was born, but, significantly, he was not misbehaving at school. Alex telling me that he was worried about his father not having an "occupation" was the clue.

Family therapy is not just a method of psychotherapy. It is a new way of looking at human behavior, of narrating the flow of events in people's lives. Rather than look for a biological "inner" cause of a child's misbehavior, we try to find another possible sequence of events, another narrative or story. Pioneer family psychiatrist Salvador Minuchin reflected in a recent interview that he learned more about being a good therapist from watching movies than from observing therapy. Minuchin tells us that the best training he ever had as a therapist was learning to create stories when he was thirteen years old. He lived in a small town in rural Argentina, right across the street from a movie house. The usher was a friend of his and would allow him to sneak into the theater at 6:00 p.m. But Minuchin's father had a strict rule that dinner was at 7:00 p.m. So after watching the movie for an hour, Minuchin would have to leave the theater and create an ending in his head. This experience "was my first training in being a psychotherapist," he says. As the narrative therapists also tell us, plays and stories teach us new possibilities. They serve as alternatives to our dominant social narratives and help us make sense of our experience in new ways.

Creating stories as a family therapist requires a shift in perspective that is not always easy to make. It took me five years of supervision and study to learn to frame sequences of human interaction like a strategic family therapist. Of course, unlike Minuchin, I didn't have to make up movie endings; when I went to the movies on Saturday afternoons, I watched them all the way through. As a family therapist, I have to identify significant events that occur at the same time that a child's problem begins—like a death, an illness, a new baby, or, in Alex's case, his father's broken arm. In sessions with children and their parents, I learned to notice that just when parents begin to argue, their child begins to act out. The child might whine. Perhaps he will run over and jump into his mother's lap. He might throw a toy on the floor, causing his parents to admonish him and apologize to me. I learned to see that a child will do just about anything to make his parents stop arguing and shift the focus of attention to himself. To grasp what is really going on with a child, I had to understand the whole sequence of family interactions of which his behavior was a part.

My teacher and mentor, Jay Haley, was fond of comparing strategic family therapy to Zen. He told the story of a university professor who visited a Zen master to learn about his spiritual practice. The master served tea. He poured his visitor's cup full, and then kept on pouring. The professor watched the overflow and exclaimed that his cup was full. The master replied: "Like this cup, you are full of your own opinions. How can I show you Zen unless you first empty your cup?" In the same way, I had to give up many of my own ways of viewing therapy clients. I had to give up thinking about individuals and began to think in terms of two or more family members.

A training video that I watched at Jay's Family Therapy Institute in Washington provided a dramatic lesson in perceiving sequences from a family therapy perspective. The video was about a young man in his twenties who used heroin. Right there in the family therapy session, whenever his parents raised their voices or talked about separating, the young man threatened to start using heroin again. I literally learned to "see" the sequences as connected. The son kept interrupting their arguments by drawing attention to his terrible problem. The task for the family therapist was, of course, to help the young man's parents become happier together so that they would stop threatening to separate. Then their son would not need to use heroin. If the therapist simply focused on the young man's heroin use out of context, there would be no improvement.

The best way of conceptualizing his heroin use, I learned, was to see that he was sacrificing himself by having a terrible problem so that his parents would stay together to help him. His parents' lives thus had a focus and a purpose; they had to help their problem son. This is not the only story one could make up about a young man's drug problem, but in this case it turned out to be a powerful instrument of change. The parents stayed together. The son stopped using heroin.

Young children have many ways of protecting their parents, and school failure is one of the big ones. If a child acts out at school or doesn't focus on his class work, his parents must put aside their own problems in order to help their child. They will have to spend time together talking about their son or daughter's problem. They will have to attend parent-teacher conferences, keep counseling appointments, and make extra visits to the pediatrician. They will need to work as a team to help their child instead of dwelling on their marital problems and thinking about getting a divorce. By deflecting the parents' attention, the child's problem protects the parents from facing their own issues.

In my experience, a child of loving parents will do almost anything to distract her parents' attention away from their own problems. Unfortunately, misbehavior is what most readily does the job. After all, reasons the child, my tantrum is a surefire way of getting my parents to focus on me; it has always worked before. As children get older, they may develop more serious problems, such as drug or alcohol use or truancy, to protect their parents and bring them to therapy.

As a rule, the more loving and caring the parents, the more their child will try to protect the parents from their own problems. For years my colleagues and I have pondered whether these attempts are conscious and deliberate or unconscious. What I learned in my early training was that younger children protect their parents unconsciously, but after age fourteen or so, the kids' efforts to help are conscious. However, in recent years I have begun to have my doubts about this. Because young children are so responsive when I say to them "Thank-you for being the helper" or "I am going to help your parents now," I have begun to think that even in a young child the intention to protect a parent is conscious.

But whether intentional or unintentional, a child's attempt to help a parent can have terrible consequences. As we have seen, in today's overmedicalized society, a child may develop a problem that will be framed as a psychiatric diagnosis such as ADHD or bipolar disorder. And that diagnosis can lead to real trouble. The child's attempted solution to the parents' problem becomes the very problem presented in therapy.

When I think that a child is having a symptom or developing problem behavior in order to help or protect a parent, my strategy is to communicate to the child that I understand what he is doing and from now on I will take over his role as the family helper. This is what I did with Alex, as well as with Joey, the little boys whom we met earlier. My goal is to see the child as little as possible in therapy—so that the child does not feel like there is something wrong with him—and work instead with the parents. Once I have reassured a child that it's my job to help his parents, there is usually no reason for the child to come to therapy sessions.

Transitions or abrupt changes in family life can trigger problems. Alex was reacting to a family transition in which the smooth narrative of his father going to work every day came to a stop. This was worrisome to Alex. His mother telling him "Daddy's cast will come off in six weeks" didn't have a clear meaning for him.

A more common reason for a child to have ADHD-like symptoms is hearing his parents argue, especially about disciplining him. Although the disagreements may not be serious, a child might secretly worry that they are a sign that his parents might separate. Even if the fantasy is unfounded, the specter of divorce has become a profound fear for children. These days 50 percent of marriages end in separation or divorce, and every child has friends whose parents are divorced.

Teachers' notes or phone calls are often the first sign that a child is having trouble. Sometimes the parents are not surprised; they've been disturbed by their son's or daughter's behavior at home. But occasionally a teacher's concern comes as a bolt out of the blue. That was the case with seven-year-old Jarrod. His second-grade teacher, Mrs. Coleman, was particularly worried because Jarrod was completely out of control in the classroom. She had been sending notes home since the beginning of the term. "Jarrod can't keep his hands to himself during recess," she reported. And worse: "He kicks or bites other students and even spit at one little girl." The teacher was especially worried because the other children were afraid of Jarrod and were starting to avoid him. And she told Jarrod's mother she'd had several complaints from other parents.

At a meeting with Mrs. Coleman, Jarrod, and his mother, Roberta, Jarrod claimed that the other boys always attacked him first and he only defended himself. But the teacher quietly insisted that Jarrod was the one who initiated the aggressive behavior. Also, she told Roberta, Jarrod was not completing his work in class and sometimes didn't even take the assignments home with him. Roberta seemed to be unaware that Jarrod wasn't turning in his worksheets, and she was distressed to learn about his kicking and biting. "Jarrod doesn't act that way at all at home," she said. Mrs. Coleman seemed unconvinced, but she was eager to help the boy. She suggested that Roberta try sitting with Jarrod and encouraging him while he did his homework. And, she added, if he did misbehave at home, Roberta might do well to try "time-outs." She also suggested that Roberta limit the amount of television that Jarrod watched at home, and to be particularly careful that he not watch television shows or play computer games with violence in them.

Roberta tried what Mrs. Coleman suggested, but the teacher reported that Jarrod was still misbehaving at school. A friend at work to whom Roberta confided about Jarrod suggested that Roberta consult me about family therapy. Roberta wasn't quite sure what this entailed, but her friend spoke so highly of how I'd helped her teenage daughter that she called me immediately.

Roberta and Jarrod came to therapy on a rainy evening in late February. Roberta, an elegant, slim woman who practiced law in a neighboring town, had come directly from work and looked tired. Jarrod was a sturdy boy, tall for his age, with a brown crew cut. He was neatly dressed in jeans and white tennis shoes with flashing red lights on the heels. He looked decidedly unhappy, the corners of his mouth slanting down. When I greeted Roberta and her son in the waiting room, Jarrod didn't want to come into my office; he hung back even when I told him there were lots of toys he might like to play with. But when Roberta leaned over and whispered something to him, he finally followed her into the office.

The first thing Jarrod wanted to know when he sat down next to his mother was if I was "a doctor who didn't give shots." I laughed and replied, "You're right, I am a doctor who doesn't give shots. No shots in my office; see for yourself." I gestured at the toy shelves.

"That's what my mom just told me," said Jarrod as he sat down on the floor to play with Lego blocks.

On the phone, Roberta had told me that she had been divorced from Jarrod's father, Tom, for two years. Her ex-husband had been emotionally abusive to her, and once he had been physically abusive as well, shoving her so hard that she fell onto a glass coffee table and shattered it. This incident prompted Roberta to move to her parents' house. She and Jarrod, who was five at the time, stayed with her parents for six months until she found a house of her own and saved up enough to pay the rent herself. Tom had custody every other weekend. Things went pretty smoothly with the co-parenting, Roberta said, but there was not much communication between her and her ex-husband.

Roberta told me about her meeting with Jarrod's teacher and Jarrod's misbehavior at school. Observing Jarrod out of the corner of my eye, I could scarcely believe that he could be the kind of bully his teacher described. He was careful with the toys, scrupulously putting the blocks away when he was finished playing with them. He had a very gentle presence for a seven-year-old boy. I was puzzled as to why this child who seemed so sweet and genial in my office turned into an aggressive bully at school. I asked Roberta if she would mind reading a magazine in the waiting room while I spent a few minutes talking with Jarrod alone.

When Roberta left, I sat down on the carpet next to Jarrod and asked him my invariant question: Was he more worried about his mother or his father. Jarrod averted his eyes, but he answered right away, "I'm worried more about my daddy. He cries when he drops me off at Mommy's house because he's sad that he doesn't have more time with me."

"Daddy cries?"

"Yes. He's really sad."

"And what about you?" I asked. "Do you want to spend more time with Daddy?"

Jarrod nodded vigorously. Then he said quietly, "But Mommy won't let me."

"Why is that?" I asked.

"Because Daddy once grabbed my arm and hurt me."

"Why did he do that?"

Jarrod hesitated and then replied very softly without looking at me, "Because he didn't know what he was doing. He was angry."

I asked Jarrod when that had happened, and he said it was a long time ago. His father had never done that again, and he had apologized to Jarrod many times over for hurting him.

I asked Jarrod about school. He liked his teacher even though he knew she got angry at him sometimes. Despite his acting out in the classroom, Jarrod did have one friend at school, Jordan. He told me that he liked to go to Jordan's house because he had a trampoline and they had fun playing on it. I was happy to hear that Jarrod had at least one friend he got along with, a hopeful sign that he wasn't always aggressive with other children.

At the end of the session, I asked Roberta to come alone to the next appointment. I wanted to find out more about Jarrod's father and his feelings about the custody arrangement. As a family therapist, I know that divorce can be hard on children, but if the parents are respectful toward each other and agree about custody, the damage to the child can be minimized.

In my session alone with Roberta, she repeated what her son had already told me: that during an argument, her ex-husband, Tom, had grabbed Jarrod's arm in frustration. What Jarrod didn't know was that the couple was in marriage counseling at the time, and when they told the marriage counselor about this incident, she reported it to Children's Services. As a consequence, Tom was allowed to have only supervised visitation for the first six months after the separation.

Once the six months were over, Tom and Roberta settled in to their arrangement for Tom to have custody of Jarrod every other weekend.

Roberta said she thought Tom had learned his lesson. He had apologized to his son and to her.

"Would Tom be willing to come to therapy to help solve Jarrod's behavior problems?" I asked. Since Jarrod had told me that he was worried about his father, I thought that his misbehavior was in some way protective of Tom. I had to figure out what Tom would need in order to be happier and see how I could bring that about.

"I think so," Roberta answered. "We don't have much communication, but I know he loves Jarrod."

Roberta had anticipated my request. She had given Tom my phone number, although she wasn't surprised that he hadn't called. "I don't think Tom believes in therapy," she said. "But if you would call him and tell him it would be good for Jarrod, that might help," she added.

I was a little hesitant since she had told me that Tom didn't believe in therapy, and calling him seemed like barging into a lion's den. But I knew that I had to get Tom to therapy in order to help Jarrod. I have called resistant fathers before because it is essential that noncustodial parents be involved if a child is having problems. Very often the custodial parent, usually the mother, doesn't want the father to be involved in the therapy. But my job description includes persuading reluctant mothers and calling antagonistic fathers.

I gathered up my courage and made the phone call to Tom. We left phone messages back and forth, but when I finally talked with him, he surprised me. He was very willing to come to therapy if it would help Jarrod.

The four of us met the following week. Tom was tall and stocky and had a gentleness about him similar to his son's. When he saw his father, Jarrod's expression changed instantly from despondency to joy. With a shout, he ran over to Tom and jumped into his lap. Tom bent over and kissed Jarrod on the top of his head; he sat for the rest of the session with his arm around Jarrod's shoulders.

Tom was defensive with me at first, presumably because he thought I would judge him harshly. But when I was friendly and respectful toward him, he slowly opened up about his resentment at seeing his son only every other weekend. He really wanted to have Jarrod for two weeks or more in the summer so they could go fishing with Tom's father, who had a cabin at a nearby mountain lake. And Tom also wanted to see Jarrod during the week so he could help him with his homework and be more a part of his life.

While Tom spoke, Roberta looked wary and tense, keeping her arms crossed defensively in front of her chest. Until now, she had refused to change the custody arrangements. She didn't seem comfortable sitting here in the room with Tom. Because of the single incident of Tom's grabbing his son's arm, the judge had awarded sole legal and physical custody to Roberta, with very limited visitation for Tom. Typically, in the absence of any unusual circumstances like abuse, child custody in California is evenly divided between the mother and the father.

I asked Roberta and Tom to come back for a session alone so we could discuss these issues without Jarrod's being present.

The couple came in later that week. They were barely seated in my office when Tom exploded. "You're just using Jarrod as a pawn to get back at me," he spat out. "You've never forgiven me for pushing you around."

Roberta was quiet and didn't interrupt, although I could see that Tom's words were difficult for her to hear.

"Maybe that's so," she said finally. "But there's no excuse for it, and there's no excuse for your hurting Jarrod. You shouldn't have grabbed his arm."

Tom was quick to speak up. "You know that was an accident. I never meant to hurt him. And I apologized right away. Jarrod forgave me right away, but you just can't get over your grudge. And you know that it's hurting Jarrod not to see me more often."

Roberta was quiet. I knew that she loved her son and had been through a lot of worry with his behavior problems. Although Jarrod's teacher hadn't mentioned a diagnosis of oppositional defiant disorder directly, Roberta knew that it was on her mind. Jarrod's pediatrician had already suggested this diagnosis as a possibility.

After talking to me and seeing the affection between Jarrod and his father, Roberta was finally beginning to realize that, for her son's sake, she needed to compromise with Tom about visitation. She also wanted Tom to be more involved with Jarrod's teacher and the school counselor about his behavior problems. She needed Tom's support in dealing with the school.

"Give the teacher my e-mail address and phone number, and tell her to keep me in the loop about Jarrod. I'll go to parent-teacher conferences or whatever it takes," said Tom.

Roberta turned to me. "Are you sure this is what's causing the problem? Are you certain there's nothing wrong with Jarrod? Do you think he might have oppositional defiant disorder or something like that?"

"The proof is in the pudding," I said. "Let's see if you and Tom having a more cordial relationship will have a positive impact on Jarrod's behavior." Based on my experience, I was sure that it would. I also knew that Roberta and Tom would have to see actual changes in Jarrod's behavior to believe that their son's real problem was their hostile relationship.

Toward the end of the session, Roberta tentatively agreed to let Tom take Jarrod on a camping trip along with Tom's father, whom she had always liked, for a week over the summer. She also agreed for Tom to have Jarrod for a week during the Easter school vacation.

So far nothing had changed with Jarrod at school. His teacher was still writing notes or e-mails home every day. But I hoped that the thawing of the parents' tensions would start to have some positive effects.

Jay Haley used to say that children's violence is always a result of conflict and tension between the child's parents. This is true whether parents are living together or divorced or separated. In a second session with Roberta and Tom alone, I convinced them of how important it was to resolve their disagreements privately and not air them in front of Jarrod. I explained that their fights made Jarrod feel terrible.

Tom told me that now he and Roberta were talking on the phone and trying to be more civil toward each other for Jarrod's sake. They were trying hard to be good parents, and there was not as much tension between them. Tom, looking at the floor sheepishly, admitted in a low voice that he had felt spiteful after the divorce. He admitted that he did try to turn Jarrod against his mother, complaining bitterly to Jarrod about his limited custody and allowing Jarrod to see him crying. Now he could see that what he had done was not in his son's best interests.

"I was being childish," Tom said candidly.

At the beginning of the fourth session, this time with Jarrod and his father, Jarrod greeted me with a big grin and excitedly told me that he had gotten gold stars from Mrs. Coleman every day that week, and got to choose a toy on Friday from the teacher's big toy basket.

"I didn't know that Mrs. Coleman gave stars," I said.

"Yes, she does. She gives everyone gold stars if they don't get into trouble. Then on Friday if you have five stars you get to pick a toy. And I didn't get into trouble once." Jarrod was clearly pleased with himself.

Tom proudly announced that there had been no notes or e-mails from Jarrod's teacher for nearly two weeks. There had not been a single incident of hitting, biting, or spitting at school. He was now picking up Jarrod from school on Wednesdays, and helping him with his homework before dinner. Jarrod was finishing his class assignments and turning them in on time.

Because Jarrod's behavior had improved so dramatically, his parents were undoubtedly using the strategies I had given them. They were no longer arguing in front of Jarrod. They were careful not to say bad things about the other parent. I asked for a telephone update in a month. At the update, both Tom and Roberta reported that Jarrod was no longer having problems at school.

Children often act out the feelings of a parent that the parent is not able to express directly. Family therapists say that the parents are communicating *indirectly through the child* because direct communication between the spouses has broken down. In Jarrod's case, his hostile behavior at school could be seen as his acting out his father's unexpressed anger at his ex-wife. The way I saw it was that Jarrod was protecting his father and also acting out his father's hostile feelings by bullying other children.

The family therapist's goal is to restore healthy, more direct communication between the parents so that their child no longer needs to be a vehicle for their exchanges. Jarrod's problems brought his parents together in therapy, where they learned to speak more amicably to each other and negotiate their needs. This process began when each of them took a respectful, nondefensive stance toward the other parent, with each of them admitting they had been wrong.

When Roberta agreed to give Tom more visitation rights, he became less angry and more cooperative. This increased visitation was actually a relief for Roberta since it gave her more time for herself. She admitted that she had fought Tom on the custody issue out of anger and spite because he had been abusive to her. With a new arrangement that made Tom much happier, Jarrod was free to improve his behavior because he did not need to protect his father anymore.

Tom and Roberta successfully made the transition from having a difficult divorce, in which they were both trying to recruit their son into siding with them, to a more civilized divorce that would not burden their son with having to take sides. As therapy researchers

Marla Isaacs, Braulio Montalvo, and David Abelsohn point out in their book *The Difficult Divorce,* couples do not have to be friends after a divorce; they need only to contain their hostility so that the children are not burdened by their ongoing anger. After divorcing, parents need to negotiate a new relationship, with their highest priority being the best interests of their children. These authors also point out the importance of both parents participating in therapy. Even though they were no longer husband and wife, Tom and Roberta were able to form a peaceful working relationship with each other for the sake of their son.

An important consideration is that a young child does not understand what divorce really means. Children often have fantasies and even dreams that their parents will get back together again. The family therapist can help a child by asking the parents to gently remind him that they will never be together as husband and wife, but they will always cooperate as parents and do what is best for him.

Both Alex and Jarrod might easily have been labeled with ADHD or a conduct disorder such as ODD. Alex's pediatrician chose to frame his behavior as acting "like a typical boy." And Jarrod's parents were eager to avoid medication and therefore willing to try a different approach to solving their child's problems.

Parents sometimes ask me what I think about giving a child a stimulant medication such as Ritalin. These parents have usually been through a lot—screaming fights at home, discouraging meetings with teachers, strains on their own relationship—and they are desperate for help. What I propose is that we try very hard to help the child with family therapy without medication. If we don't see significant improvement after four or five sessions of family therapy, then the parents are of course welcome to pursue other avenues of treatment. I have found that if parents respond well to my interventions—such as being careful not to argue or disagree with each other in front of their child and to shelter their child from problems in their own lives—they will be well on their way to avoiding medication.

I never refuse to see a child who is already taking medication if the parents want to try family therapy. But often parents bring a child to me when medication is no longer helping and their doctor fears that increasing the dosage might produce harmful side effects. This was the situation with Laura, whom we met in Chapter 2. Laura was already taking medications for ADHD, anxiety, and depression when I first met her. I suggested that her mother try family therapy to supplement the medication for a couple of months, at the end of which time we would reevaluate.

With Laura, the outcome was positive and she was able to do well without medication. But like any other therapist, I am not successful with every case. No matter how hard I try, not every family therapy story has a happy ending. I recall a nine-year-old boy named Justin who was distracted and disruptive in his classroom, and aggressive with other students. He also wet the bed at night. Justin's parents had been through a difficult divorce. The father had custody of Justin and the mother had custody of Justin's twin sister, Julia.

The parents refused to come to therapy together to discuss how to help Justin, and they refused to talk to each other, even to arrange visitations. Justin hadn't seen his sister or his mother for over a year. Although both parents trusted me, I was not successful in getting them to put aside their angry feelings and negotiate a cooperative co-parenting relationship. I even met with both sets of grandparents and tried to get them to mediate between the parents. But nothing worked. Justin was eventually diagnosed with ODD and ADHD and was put on Adderall—which did help calm him down and focus better at school. I often wonder if he ever saw his mother or his twin sister again.

FOUR

Metaphor

ARLY FAMILY THERAPISTS like Jay Haley and his colleagues on the Bateson communication project were interested in communication on many different levels. They noticed that people in therapy often used language metaphorically or poetically, bestowing more than one meaning on a word or a statement. Jay believed that if a mother told the therapist that her son was obstinate, the odds were that the mother was also saying that her husband was being obstinate. Or if a father said his child was threatening to run away, he might also mean that his wife was threatening to leave him.

The standard definition of metaphor is "a comparison without using 'like' or 'as.'" An example is Shakespeare's famous phrase "All the world's a stage." Family therapists use the word in a slightly different way, to signify the way language transports our thinking from one level of meaning to another. In fact, this is the original definition of metaphor, which comes from the Greek *metapherin*, meaning to carry over or transport. In Hamlet's line "To sleep perchance to dream," the word "sleep" transports our minds, as well as Hamlet's mind, from the level of everyday sleeping and dreaming to a deeper level. In the context of the play, we know that to the tormented young prince, "sleep" also means "death."

A family therapist must move smoothly between levels of meaning in the family, and it is metaphor that allows us to do this. It transports us from the plane of the individual symptom to the level of the deeper problem in the family system. This is why metaphor has been so crucially important to family therapy from its earliest beginnings in Bateson's communication project.

When I am doing therapy, I'm thinking of two levels of meaning all the time. If a child is angry and explosive, I immediately ask myself who else in his family might be angry and explosive, even though the other family member may express those feelings in a different fashion. We saw this with Joey, whose outward anger reflected his father's inner rage about his job. If an adolescent is cutting herself, to take a more serious example, I ask myself who else in her family is being self-destructive. When, as in the case of the Torres family that we meet below, a father says, "She gets everything she wants by having tantrums," he is literally referring to his daughter. But he may also be talking about his wife and obliquely about the imbalance of power in his marriage.

Just as patients speak on two levels of meaning at once, therapists must be able to move from the literal level to the metaphorical and sometimes vice versa. Early strategic therapists like Milton Erickson often used metaphor to get around a patient's reluctance to address a particular subject. One of Erickson's most famous examples concerned a schizophrenic young man in a mental hospital who insisted that he was Jesus Christ. One day, Erickson approached him on the hospital grounds and said, "I understand you have had experience as a carpenter." The patient had to say he had. Erickson was then able to involve him in building a bookcase and later on in more productive labor, which turned out to be very therapeutic.

Here Erickson moved from the metaphorical level to the literal level, instead of the other way around. The patient, in claiming he was Jesus Christ, was metaphorically communicating his profound suffering. Erickson, well aware of this metaphorical use of language, did not want to dwell on the young man's pain. Instead, by interpreting the patient's statement literally, he was able to help him do something productive. This kind of intervention is typical of Erickson's core belief that taking action was always more valuable than dwelling interminably on painful feelings. He was so opposed to talking about emotions with his patients that when one woman started to cry in a therapy session, he said, as he passed her the tissue box, "At Christmastime we have green tissues." The woman's laughter produced a change in her mood much more quickly than focusing on her sadness would have done.

Metaphor played an important part in my treatment of the Torres family. The parents, distraught about their daughter's extreme anxiety, consulted me after their pediatrician told them she thought the cause of the anxiety was probably emotional.

When I first greeted Cindy and her parents in the waiting room, I was struck by the resemblance between mother and daughter. Kara, the mother, was tall and dark complexioned, with frightened black eyes and thick dark brown hair tumbling to her shoulders. Cindy, at age ten, was also tall, with the same thick hair as her mother and the same frightened look in her eyes. Cindy's father was sitting across from them, engrossed in his laptop computer.

"You must be the Torres family," I said warmly. With a smile, I looked in the daughter's direction, and added, "And you must be Cindy. Please come in."

"What can I do for you?" I asked when everyone was seated in my office.

"Well," began Cindy's father, Brent, closing his laptop, "Cindy has been feeling anxious for about two years, but lately it's been getting worse. Two weeks ago, she was feeling so much anxiety that she vomited while she was visiting my mother for the weekend. We had to drive there and pick her up."

While her father was talking, Cindy fidgeted with a button on her red cardigan. The button was dangling by a single thread.

Kara interjected, "Hasn't her anxiety been going on for more like three years? I remember she was feeling really awful at your sister's wedding. I almost had to stay home with her."

"Maybe it's been three years," Brent said, looking annoyed.

"And has it been getting worse?" I asked, noting the minor discord that had sprung up between the parents. They seemed to be at odds with each other even about the smallest details. Did this mean that there was a more significant source of tension between them? Perhaps Cindy's anxiety reflected the strain between her parents, or perhaps her anxiety was metaphorically expressing one parent's anxiety. Thinking in terms of more than one person makes it easier for a therapist to bring about change. Jay Haley used to advise therapists that they will produce the most change in a family if they work with at least three people.

In answer to my question about Cindy's problems getting worse, Kara said, "Yes. Now she refuses to go to Brent's mother's house because she says she feels too anxious there. She's scared that she'll vomit again."

"I see," I said, jotting this down in my notepad. Then I turned to Cindy and asked, "What helps you feel better when you're feeling anxious?" Cindy thought about this for a few seconds, wrinkling her brow.

"I feel better when Mommy or Daddy is close by."

"Okay. That makes sense. You feel better when one of your parents is with you."

Here, I was reflecting her feeling so that she would hear that I understood her.

I turned to Kara. "Is Cindy having any other problems?"

"She has tantrums if she doesn't get her way," Kara said after a short pause.

"And how do you handle them?"

"Brent is stern with her, but I have more patience." This conversation was clearly making Cindy uncomfortable. By now, she had torn off the button on her sweater and was rolling it around in her hand.

Brent interjected, pointing at his wife, "She gives in too easily. She gives Cindy anything she wants, anything to get her to stop screaming."

"That's not exactly true," Kara retorted, anger rising in her voice.

"You give in to her most of the time."

"I understand," I said. I needed to change the subject and stop the arguing. Hearing her parents fighting was not good for Cindy. I also wanted to learn more about this family. I decided to ask Kara and Brent how they had met. I often pose this question to couples, because recapturing joyful memories of their courtship can make them feel closer in the present. Kara and Brent told me they'd met at an insurance company where they both were working and they dated for two years before getting married. It was a second marriage for Brent; he had an older son who was away at college.

I then asked about their parents and extended families. Kara's parents were retired and lived nearby, and Brent's widowed mother lived about an hour away.

"What would help me now is to speak with Cindy alone for a few minutes," I told the parents.

When Kara and Brent had left the room, I asked Cindy to tell me about her activities. She said that she played basketball on the school team and also took ballet lessons. She told me about the new kitten named Cassie that she got for her birthday. When she was feeling comfortable with me, I asked her gently, "Are you worried about your parents?"

"My father *hates* my grandmother," she burst out. "And, and…," she stammered, "I'm afraid my parents will get a divorce because they're always fighting about Grandma. That's my mother's mother," she said, adding that she called her father's mother "Nana."

"Daddy doesn't want Grandma and Poppy to come to dinner. I don't know why." She began to cry softly. I handed Cindy a tissue.

"Cindy, I'm going to be the one to help your parents now. Please don't worry. I'll meet with them alone and help them solve the problem about Grandma. That's my job. I'm sure it's not as bad as you think. Besides, I've helped parents with much worse problems."

She looked at me tearfully and asked if I was sure that I could help them. Her parents' problems seemed so magnified and terrible in her mind. I reassured Cindy that I would be the professional family helper now.

"That would be good," she said with a nod.

I thought to myself that no wonder this little girl was feeling so anxious. She was caught in the middle of a heated conflict in her family. I needed to explore this issue with her parents.

I reached into a drawer of my desk and brought out a small spiral-bound notebook with a picture on the cover of a kitten tangled in a ball of yarn. I keep a supply of these notebooks in my desk.

"Here," I said to Cindy, "this can be your worry notebook. Whenever you feel upset or anxious, just write down the time and place and how you're feeling. It will help you feel better. Later on, I'll look at it with you."

"Thanks," she said. She carefully printed her name on the first page. Underneath her name, she printed "My Worry Book."

When Cindy was calmer, I invited Brent and Kara back in to join us. I said I would like to meet with them alone in the next session.

"Don't you want to see Cindy again?" Kara asked, surprised. I hear this from a lot of parents. They understandably assume that the child is the one with the problem.

"Of course," I said, "but in the next session it would be best for me to meet with you and your husband alone." We made an appointment for the following week.

I was beginning to form a hypothesis that Cindy's intense anxiety was a metaphor for another level of anxiety in her family, somehow involving her grandmothers. Perhaps there was an issue about parent-grandparent boundaries. The role of grandparents is to give advice and counsel when asked—and only when asked—and to lend a help-ing hand with the grandchildren if the parents ask them for help. But when grandparents become intrusive in the life of the nuclear fam-ily, a child may well become symptomatic. Often the intrusiveness is combined with an overly close relationship between a wife and her mother. Was this happening in Cindy's family?

In the session with Kara and Brent, they told me that Cindy com-plained all week that she was feeling anxious. One day she refused to go to school because she said she was afraid she'd throw up.

"Do you think she has an anxiety disorder?" Kara asked me in a worried tone.

Unfortunately, this was not the first time that a parent had asked me this question. Children are all too frequently diagnosed with anxi-ety disorders. A 1999 study by the U.S. Department of Health and Human Services found that each year as many as one in eight children between the ages of nine and seventeen are diagnosed as suffering from generalized anxiety disorder or social anxiety disorder or school phobia. The psychiatric medications of choice for treating children with severe anxiety are the selective serotonin reuptake inhibitors (SSRIs), such as Prozac, Zoloft, and Paxil.

Viewing children's situational anxiety as a psychiatric disor-der is only one more example of the trend toward medicalizing their problems without looking at alternatives. Many parents don't understand that there is a difference between a child's becoming anxious or worried because of an uncomfortable situation—parents fighting, a mean teacher, a bullying classmate—and having a "disorder," which suggests that the child has some sort of biological impairment.

I reassured Kara. "Sometimes children respond to family situations by feeling anxious. So I'd like to explore that a little. It doesn't mean that Cindy has a biological disorder. It means only that certain situations are troubling to her and may cause her to feel worried. Since Cindy had that severe attack of anxiety and nausea at her grandmother's house, that situation would be a good place to start. That was your mother's house?" I asked, looking at Brent.

He nodded.

"What about your mother?" I asked Kara. "Does Cindy ever feel anxious at her house?"

"No," Kara said.

"Cindy sees your mother more often?"

Brent burst out, "We see Kara's parents *all the time*. They're always dropping in at our house. Sometimes they don't even call first to tell us they're coming. And they take Cindy on vacations that we can't possibly afford. Last year they took her to Hawaii. The year before, it was England. It's not that I didn't want Cindy to go. I want her to have these experiences. But I feel bad that I can't afford to take my family on nice vacations."

Kara looked tense at hearing such a strong display of emotion about her parents.

"I'm tired of your parents calling the shots in our family," Brent continued.

"What?" Kara asked, obviously stunned.

"Every time you want something for Cindy that we can't afford, you just go to your parents and ask for the money. How do you think that makes me feel? It's emasculating."

There was a tense pause. I looked down at the carpet, focusing on a stain I hadn't noticed before. I'd have to mention it to the cleaning crew.

Kara broke the silence.

"I thought we agreed that we'd accept help from my parents because Cindy wanted ballet lessons so badly. The shoes and costumes were so expensive."

"I might have agreed at the time. But I'm getting sick and tired of their paying for things. And I'm sick of you inviting them to stay for dinner every time they drop in. I need to have some privacy in my own home. I'm the *man* of the house."

Brent went on, his voice rising now. "And I don't like you talking to them about us and our marriage. They always take your side, and say things like 'we told you not to marry him' or 'you could have done much better than Brent.' How do you think that makes me feel? And you want us to spend every holiday with them. Sometimes I think you would rather be married to your parents than to me."

Kara looked stunned and hurt. Tears were welling up in her eyes. She glanced over at me, as if asking for support.

"That's not true at all," she said.

"Kara, it's good that Brent is able to express these feelings. His anger may be affecting Cindy and contributing to her anxiety. But I know that hearing his anger is difficult for you. Maybe we could work out some kind of compromise."

"My mother helps us so much. And my father comes over to fix things if Brent isn't around. Just last week Brent was out of town and our air-conditioning broke. My father came right over and fixed it."

"I would have fixed it if I were home. You know that," Brent said angrily.

"But you were in Cincinnati. And it was over ninety-five degrees here."

The session was nearly over. I was beginning to see that my hunch had been correct. Kara's parents were overly critical of Brent—at least in Brent's eyes—and they were causing trouble in the couple's marriage. I needed to calm things down before they left.

"I'm sure we can work this out," I said soothingly.

Then I turned to Kara. "Maybe you could just think about what Brent said. It would be best not to change anything right now. And please don't discuss this at home where Cindy might overhear you. Hearing you argue will upset her."

Brent and Cindy looked at the floor.

I went on. "Brent, I understand your feelings, and we'll negotiate some changes. But first I'd like you to say just one nice thing about Kara's mother in front of Cindy this week. Cindy needs to hear that from you."

"If you think it would help Cindy," Brent said with a sigh. Then he added, "I want Cindy to be able to visit my mother's house without so much drama."

"Don't worry, we'll arrange that. I promise. The main thing right now is for Cindy to see you and Kara getting along peacefully."

We made an appointment for the two of them to come in the following week. Now the source of Cindy's anxiety was becoming clearer to me. She felt caught between her parents. And Kara felt caught between her husband and her parents. Cindy's anxiety was a metaphor for her mother's anxiety.

Children caught in the cross fire between parents over a grandparent often develop feelings of anxiety or even worse symptoms, especially if they feel they have to take sides. And Cindy was clearly taking her mother's side in this battle. I could now see that Cindy's rejection of Brent's mother reflected Brent's rejection of Kara's mother.

At the beginning of the next session, Kara announced that Cindy was feeling a little bit better.

"She's gone to school all week. And she's been writing in her worry notebook."

Kara had even taken the initiative and called her mother, saying a few tactful words about how she and Brent needed a little more privacy at home. The call made Kara anxious because she was afraid of hurting her mother's feelings. But she had done it. Kara told me that her mother was surprised, and protested, saying she never knew that Kara felt that way and reminding her how much she loved buying Cindy gifts and taking her on vacation. She had no idea that this might make Brent feel bad.

"I want our marriage to be happy," Kara said, looking at Brent. "I know we have some issues, but that's why we're here—to sort them out."

The couple's fights ran the usual gamut. Brent wanted Kara to go back to work, at least part-time, so they could have enough money for vacations and a new car. Kara liked staying home so she could be there for Cindy after school. She wanted to have another baby; Brent didn't. Kara also allowed Cindy to come into their bed when she woke up in the middle of the night. Brent thought that Cindy should sleep in her own bed.

"And did Brent say a nice thing about your mother in Cindy's presence?" I asked. I wanted to keep the focus on their complying with my suggestions.

"He did," admitted Kara, looking at Brent. "He complimented the strawberry jam that she made for us. He told Cindy that it was very special to have Grandma's homemade jam."

It was time to broach the topic of the other grandmother. I turned to Kara and asked her how she felt about Cindy's relationship with Brent's mother, whose name was Olga.

"I feel that Olga is too strict with Cindy. She's very rigid about rules. Dinner has to be at a certain time. Cindy has to eat everything on her plate. That's really hard for her because she's such a picky eater."

"That's because you've indulged her so much. You've allowed her to be picky," Brent said, his voice rising again. Then he added, "My mother is very reasonable about rules. She doesn't allow Cindy to manipulate her into getting her way all the time. In our house, she gets whatever she wants."

As he was saying this, Brent covered his mouth with his hand—suggesting to me that he had more to say on this subject. I thought that Brent might be metaphorically referring to his wife as well as his daughter when he said, "*She* gets whatever she wants." As I mentioned above, often what a father says about his child is a metaphor for what he is thinking, but not comfortable saying directly, about his wife. Did Brent feel that Kara got everything she wanted? I asked myself. Against his wishes they spent most holidays with his wife's parents, and, despite his urging, Kara refused to go back to work. I was sure that Brent felt disempowered in their marriage.

"When are you planning your next visit to Brent's mother?" I asked.

"Her birthday is in two weeks. I'd like us to visit then. She's invited us for dinner," Brent said.

I glanced at Kara. Her lips were drawn tightly together.

"Perhaps you could help Cindy pick out a card and a gift for her nana," I suggested to Kara. "Could you and Cindy bake her a birthday cake or make cupcakes?"

After a pause, Kara responded.

"That might work. Cindy loves to help me bake." Another pause. And then she continued. "But she doesn't want to go to Olga's house."

Was Kara also metaphorically saying that *she* didn't want to go to her mother-in-law's house?

"I think it would help if you expressed enthusiasm about the trip and told her that you wanted the whole family to go."

"I could do that, I guess. I know it would make Brent happy," Kara said.

"I think that would be very important," I said firmly.

With Kara encouraging her, Cindy agreed to visit Nana for her birthday, though she wanted to be sure that Kara would stay next to her the whole time they were there. As it turned out, the trip went smoothly, without Cindy feeling anxious. We were all relieved.

I worked with Brent and Kara for five months. After the first three sessions, we met every two weeks. My goal was to correct the imbalance of power in their marriage and also give Brent a voice in the way they dealt with Cindy's tantrums and discipline issues in general.

Kara made small strides at standing up to her parents. She asked them to call before dropping by their house, and she didn't automatically invite them to stay for dinner when they were there. As his in-laws showed more respect for their privacy, Brent's angry feelings toward them softened.

Brent talked to his own mother about relaxing the rules around dinner when Cindy was visiting. This wasn't easy for Olga—she was set in her ways, and, having been a widow for six years, she'd gotten used to routines that suited her but not necessarily Cindy or even Brent and Kara. Cindy did agree to visit Brent's mother as long as Kara went with her and stayed close.

As the tension between Cindy's parents eased, Cindy's anxiety decreased. I checked in with Kara a month after their last session, and she said that Cindy hadn't complained of anxiety at all since they last saw me.

A child's problem is often a reflection of a marriage problem, as we saw with Cindy. With a single parent, the child's problem can be a metaphorical expression of the parent's anxiety or sadness. That was the case with eleven-year-old Laura, whom we met earlier. Laura was in such despair that she had threatened to kill herself. But a child's distress can even reflect the problem of another member of the family—such as a sibling. And this isn't always obvious right away.

That's why I need to become familiar with all aspects of a child's story in order to reveal the metaphor and figure out what is troubling the child on the level of the family system.

Interpreting the metaphor in eight-year-old Cora's family was an interesting challenge. Cora had always been a joy to her parents. She was a straight-A student and sang in the church choir. When Cora suddenly started to fail tests and not do her homework, her parents were devastated. They could not understand why their angel was suddenly doing poorly at school. Cora didn't have a clue about why she was failing, and neither did the pediatrician. He checked Cora's vision and hearing and, finding nothing wrong, suggested that therapy might be helpful.

Cora's parents brought her to my office late one afternoon in autumn. When I greeted the family in the waiting room, Cora's father was reading to her from a *Harry Potter* book. Cora, a sweet-faced girl with blond braids, sat very close to her father and looked thoroughly engrossed in the story. Cora's mother was thumbing through a magazine, her brows knitted together in a worried look. I introduced myself, smiling at Cora. We all shook hands and I invited them into my office. Cora sat on the couch between her mother, Helena, and her father, Tim. When I gently asked Cora why she wasn't trying at school anymore, her blue eyes brimmed with tears.

"I feel like such a loser," she said, a tear rolling down her cheek.

I was surprised. I had never heard an eight-year-old girl refer to herself as a "loser." Did she hear this from her teacher or someone at school? I hoped not, but I decided to explore this route.

"Do you like your teacher?" I asked her.

Cora nodded. "She's very nice."

Helena added that the teacher was in the dark about why Cora had suddenly started to fail.

For the moment, I dropped the subject of Cora's schoolwork and asked her to tell me a little more about her family. Cora said that she had an older sister named Penny and an older brother named Phillip. I asked the parents about their jobs, since sometimes a child's failing at school can be a metaphor for a parent's failure at work. But both Tim and Helena were doing well. Tim's small advertising company, which he had started five years ago, was prospering. Helena had just gotten a promotion at the nonprofit agency where she worked as a fund-raiser. They both loved their jobs.

OK, I thought to myself. It's time for a more direct tactic. Jay Haley used to ask: "What would be the consequence for the family if the child got better? Would the family then have a much bigger problem to worry about?" I needed to answer these questions for myself.

"If Cora were doing fine at school, what would be the biggest problem in your family?" I asked. Helena and Tim looked at each other, puzzled.

"I mean, what's your second-biggest problem now?" I clarified.

Helena answered, with tears gathering in her eyes, "I guess it would be Phillip." Tim nodded in agreement.

And then she told me the story, with Tim interjecting a few comments here and there. Phillip, who was twenty-three, recently lost his latest job. He had dropped out of college after his first year and had worked at a series of dead-end jobs, each of which lasted less than a year. He was still living at home and was a great worry to his parents, who said he had a brilliant mind and a lot of potential. They couldn't bear the thought that their talented son was failing in life.

"So Phillip is the 'loser?'" I asked, glancing at Cora.

"I shouldn't have said that," Tim admitted, averting his eyes. Tim had lost his temper after Phillip had been fired from his latest job and called his son a "loser." Cora apparently had overheard him.

Now I had a good hunch. Maybe Cora's falling short at school was a metaphor for a much more serious failure in their family. Was

Cora failing in order to distract her parents from the problem of her brother? Was she protecting them, in much the same way that Joey, Alex, and Jarrod protected their parents? This seemed likely to me.

I turned to Cora and assured her that I would meet with her parents and Phillip and help her brother resolve his problems. After all, I told her, he still had lots of time to turn his life around.

"Meanwhile," I added, looking at Cora, "your job is to do well at school and not worry about your brother or your parents."

I made a few other suggestions to Cora. She could bring her mother a glass of juice when she came home from work or make her a card or picture at school. I was here substituting healthy ways that Cora could be helpful to her mother instead of having problems with her schoolwork. Cora liked these ideas. But to really help Cora, I would have to help Phillip get back on track.

At the end of the family session, I asked Tim and Helena if they would like to bring Phillip to therapy. Yes, they said, obviously relieved that I wanted to meet with their son. They didn't even ask me how this would help Cora. Somehow, they seemed to know that Phillip's situation might be affecting the whole family.

I was actually surprised that Phillip was willing to come to therapy. The way his parents described him, he sounded oppositional and withdrawn, not especially eager to reach out for help. When Helena brought Phillip to the session (Tim was out of town on a business trip), I was surprised by his wholesome, clean-cut appearance. He shook hands with me politely and looked me in the eye when I greeted him and his mother in the waiting room. What a nice young man, I thought to myself.

As I usually do when I see an adolescent or young adult, I gave Phillip the choice of having his mother in the session or speaking with me alone. He said he'd prefer to talk with me alone, and Helena said she was happy to catch up on some work in the waiting room. She had brought her laptop.

Without much prompting, Phillip told me that he was sad ever since his girlfriend, Dale, broke up with him eight months ago. They had been dating since their senior year in high school. They went to different colleges and saw each other on vacations. But during their first year in college, Dale had started to draw away from him. As he spoke, Phillip began to weep.

"And you dated off and on until eight months ago?" I asked gently.

"Yes." Phillip took a tissue from the box on the table next to him. He blew his nose and wiped his eyes.

"Dale said she thought we should date other people. I was her first boyfriend and she was my first girlfriend, and she thought we both needed more experience. I got really upset, and I couldn't concentrate at work. I was working for the park service as a lifeguard. It was a great job, but I couldn't stand to be alone in the tower for hours and hours. All I could think about was Dale. So I stopped showing up for work, and finally they fired me." Now he was crying again.

I let Phillip express his pain. I was sympathetic and encouraging. I pointed out that he was young and attractive. He had a loving family that cared about him. He was very intelligent. Some grief was natural and to be expected, but when he was finished grieving, he would surely find another girlfriend.

And another job, I hope, I said to myself.

"I feel really bad about causing my parents so much trouble."

"They just want you to feel better and move on with your life."

"I know. I need to find a job, and start taking college classes."

"Good idea."

"What about friends?" I asked him. Close friends are an important source of support for a young person trying to recover from a bad breakup. Phillip said he thought that his friends might help him.

After this first session, Phillip started to feel a little better. In my view, his sad feelings were situational—natural feelings of bereavement at the loss of his girlfriend. I didn't think he was clinically depressed, and since he didn't mention antidepressant medication, neither did I.

I met with Phillip two more times. Even though jobs were scarce, he was able to land an internship, with modest pay but good training, providing technical support for a small architectural firm. He liked the job because it kept him busy all day, and he didn't have any time to dwell on Dale.

I also met with Tim and Helena to work on their relationship. I believed that the issues between them had to be resolved before Phillip was able to think about moving out of the house. This is not at all unusual. Sometimes young adults think they need to stay home to give their parents a focus and a reason to stay together if they are not getting along. Many parents have said to me, "Our kid's problems have made us closer."

At the heart of Tim and Helena's conflict was the fact that twelve years before, Tim had had a flirtation—not a real affair—with a colleague. Phillip used to hear his parents fighting about this. They had gone to marriage counseling and worked things out, but now and then they still had arguments and Helena would bring up the past. Phillip still secretly feared that they would divorce.

For our final family session, I devised a scenario and spoke to Phillip's parents ahead of time to enlist their cooperation. In the session, Tim and Helena reassured Phillip convincingly that they were happy in their marriage. They told him that they had signed up to take dance classes together every Saturday afternoon. They were also looking forward to a cruise in the summer; Helena's parents would stay at their house with Cora and Penny. Equally important, they told him that they had confidence in him and expected him to do well.

Phillip eventually started to date a nice young woman named Beth, whom he had known in high school. Since he wanted more privacy to be with Beth, that spring he moved out of his parents' house into an apartment of his own. He had been given a raise at his technical support job, and he'd signed up to take computer science classes at a local community college two nights a week.

In addition to helping Phillip and his and Cora's parents, I made one small intervention with Cora early on to help her do better at school. Cora's parents agreed that if she got A's at the end of the semester, they would take her and a friend to Disneyland. If she got less than B's, then Helena was going to go to school with her for a day—and she convinced Cora that she really meant it. Cora was embarrassed at the thought of her mother accompanying her to school. And the Disneyland offer was enticing. Cora soon bounced back to being a straight-A student.

With some kinds of problems, I have to intervene at the level of the individual as well as at the level of the family system. I met with Phillip to help him recover from his sadness over the loss of his girlfriend. I gave Cindy a notebook to log her anxieties while I worked with her parents to resolve the family system problem.

With a twelve-year-old girl named Elizabeth, I once again had to work at two levels: the child and the family system. Like Cindy, Elizabeth was severely anxious. But Elizabeth attempted to control her anxiety with a repetitive and apparently compulsive behavior: frequently washing her hands. In fact, Elizabeth's pediatrician had diagnosed her with OCD (obsessive-compulsive disorder). When Elizabeth's mother, Debbie, called me to make an appointment, she told me that her daughter was always worried about getting sick and washed her hands at least twenty times a day.

Debbie was in her early forties and more than a little overweight. Both she and her husband, Steve, had kind eyes and both looked worried. Debbie twisted a tissue in her hands. Steve stared glumly at the floor in front of him. He worked in the shipping department of a manufacturing company. Debbie had sold handmade quilts at crafts bazaars and flea markets until about a year ago. But they were having a hard time making ends meet, so Debbie took a full-time job at a nearby assembly plant.

Elizabeth was in middle school. She was tall for her age, with short copper-colored hair and hazel eyes. She wore blue jeans and a bright aqua T-shirt. I noticed that her fingernails were chewed down to the quick.

Debbie said that Elizabeth had always been a "worrywart" and a bit of a hypochondriac. "Kind of like her mother," she added.

"So you're a worrier too?" I asked Debbie. She nodded and told me that she took medication for her anxiety and for her ulcer. I was beginning to form a tentative hypothesis that Elizabeth's anxiety might be a metaphor for her mother. After all, Debbie had made a point of telling me that her daughter was a "worrywart" and a "hypochondriac" like herself.

Steve told me that Elizabeth was incessantly asking them questions about getting sick: "If I play in the park, will my hands get contaminated? Will getting dirt on my hands give me salmonella?" No matter how much they reassured her, the questions continued—and so did the compulsive hand washing.

Elizabeth's fears had begun about a year ago, around the time Debbie went back to work. I wondered if that had anything to do with her problem. I would have to talk to Elizabeth alone to get a better picture.

When her parents left the room, I asked Elizabeth whether she was more worried about her mother or her father. I wanted to find out if she was being helpful to one of her parents by her endless questions about getting sick. Such a myriad of questions could certainly serve to distract parents from their own problems. She answered with no hesitation.

"I'm worried about my mom. She comes home from work at ten thirty at night and I'm afraid she'll get hit by a drunk driver. There are a lot of drunk drivers on the big street near our house. And it's really dark on our street. There are no street lamps." She was speaking faster and faster, an edge to her voice. "And Mom's always so worried about money. I wish she wouldn't work so much. And she eats too much junk food. Her doctor says she should go on a diet." Elizabeth explained that her mother had high blood pressure and a stomach ulcer.

I reassured her that I would meet with her mother alone and see how I could help her.

Then I focused on Elizabeth's hand washing. I decided to use a technique called the "strategic dialogue" that I learned from the Italian strategic therapist Giorgio Nardone. I often use this technique with children or teenagers who have compulsive behaviors. I ask the children questions that take me deeper into their experience and make them feel understood and accepted.

I asked Elizabeth whether she washed her hands with hot or cold water, whether she washed in the kitchen or in the bathroom, whether she used soap or not, and whether she dried her hands with a towel. Elizabeth, intrigued by my questions and my interest in her, replied that she washed with cold water and used soap. She usually washed in the bathroom and she dried her hands with a towel. Together, we explored all aspects of her hand washing. I wanted Elizabeth to know that I accepted her just as she was and wanted to fully understand her experience of washing her hands. Only by accepting and not judging her odd behavior would I be able to help her. Trying to limit her hand washing would not help at all.

After ten minutes of this dialogue, Elizabeth unexpectedly burst out: "I don't wash my hands at the beach. The beach is a happy place. I wish we could go to the beach more often." When Elizabeth started to talk about the beach, the expression on her face changed from drawn and worried to smiling. It was like the sun coming out of the clouds on a rainy day. Her father was teaching her to surf, she told me. And he sometimes took her to the beach early in the mornings before he went to work. On weekends, the whole family often went to the beach. Was there anywhere else where she didn't wash her hands so much? I asked her. She thought about this for a few moments, and then answered, "I don't wash them so much at school, or when I'm at a friend's house."

Our time was almost up, so I invited Steve and Debbie back into my office. I gave Elizabeth a little notebook so she could write down the exact places and times that she felt the most anxiety. If she had any questions about health issues, I told her to write them in the notebook as well. And I told her that, at the end of each day, she was allowed to pose two questions from the notebook to each of her parents. Elizabeth agreed. Her parents, visibly relieved, said this would help a lot. They could each handle two questions a day.

Then I prescribed a paradoxical strategy, similar to the one I prescribed for the parents of Joey when he had so much trouble going to sleep. I asked Debbie to supervise Elizabeth's hand washing in the following way. For each time Elizabeth washed her hands more than twice a day, she had to wash her hands eight times. Debbie was to stay in the bathroom with Elizabeth until she was finished. She was to remind her to use plenty of soap and be sure she rinsed it all off.

The idea behind prescribing the very behavior that we wanted to stop was to make having the behavior more troublesome for Elizabeth than stopping it. With her mother giving her directions, Elizabeth would soon get mighty tired of washing her hands. Repetitive behaviors like hand washing fall into two categories: they are either attempts to prevent something from happening in the future or attempts to repair something from the past. With Elizabeth, her hand washing was preventative. She washed her hands in order to prevent germs from making her sick. A fourteen-year-old girl whom I treated provided an example of a reparative compulsive behavior. In the hours she was at home, she repetitively opened and closed her bedroom door. Her mother had died when she was only four, and she told me that closing the door somehow made her feel connected to her mother.

I made an appointment to see Debbie alone the following week. Since Elizabeth was mainly worried about her mother's health and didn't mention anything about her parents arguing or having other problems, I thought it would be best to work with her mother.

When we met, Debbie reported that Elizabeth's hand washing was "a little bit better." The strategy was helping; Elizabeth had been asking her parents fewer questions. I then turned to Debbie's health. She agreed she needed to cut out junk food and thought it would be good to get more exercise. Like many parents, Debbie wondered what her own health had to do with her daughter. I explained that it was common for a daughter to worry about her mother. Debbie thought that this was strange. But, at my suggestion, she agreed not to let Elizabeth overhear her talking on the phone about her medical problems, and to make a stronger commitment to losing weight.

We also talked about her coming home from work late at night. Debbie acknowledged that Elizabeth was so worried that sometimes she would walk up and down the street until her mother drove into the driveway. Debbie had requested a daytime shift, but that was going to take another month or so. I asked her to reassure her daughter in the meantime that she was a very safe driver. I also asked her to tell Elizabeth two positive things about her day.

"That's a tough one," Debbie said. "My days just kind of go by."

"Then you will have to plan some good things for yourself so you can tell Elizabeth about them," I said. "You can take a short walk with a co-worker during your break. You can plan something fun for yourself on the weekend. This is very important. Elizabeth must hear good things about your life," I insisted. "And she must hear that you are eating healthy food."

When I saw Elizabeth again two weeks later, I was pleased to see she seemed a little happier. We went over her notebook together, but she hadn't written much down. She was feeling better and logging only two or three questions a day. She didn't feel she had to wash her hands as frequently, she reported. She was now washing only four or five times a day.

I continued to see Elizabeth—sometimes alone and sometimes with her parents—twice a month for the next five months, about nine sessions in all. Debbie was finally able to change to a daytime shift. She was walking two miles every morning and avoiding junk food. She was also careful to not complain about her health when her daughter could overhear her. Elizabeth's hand washing became less and less frequent. She stopped asking her parents so many questions, and was very excited to tell me that she was becoming a "really good surfer."

Children's anxieties and fears often emerge from situations in their families that are stressful to them. Elizabeth was worried about her mother's health, so she repeatedly asked her parents questions about illness. She felt most compelled to wash her hands at home, where her worries about her mother were strongest. Helping Elizabeth discover situations where she did not wash her hands or washed them less often—when she was at the beach or at school—began to give her a sense of mastery over her actions. I framed her anxiety and compulsion as temporary behaviors that occurred under some circumstances and not others, rather than as permanent qualities in her biological makeup.

Repetitive hand washing is viewed as a classic symptom of the psychiatric disorder OCD. Often children with this behavior are prescribed medication. When a parent tells me that their child has been diagnosed with OCD or some other psychiatric disorder, I don't argue with them. I accept it as a "presumed" or tentative diagnosis. Instead of trying to find more symptoms that confirm a diagnosis of OCD, I take each problem behavior and look for contexts in which it does not occur or occurs less often.

This technique is related to an important family therapy concept called "the exception," which was created by the solution-focused school of family therapy. Exceptions are times or places when the problem behavior does not occur, where the child feels and behaves as though she were normal and happy. With Elizabeth, I learned that the problem surfaced "except" when she was at the beach. Then we found two more exceptions: when she was at school or at a friend's house. Exceptions are important because they show us that what looks like a compulsive or an involuntary behavior is actually under the child's control in certain situations. In fact, as a family therapist, I generally assume that all problem behaviors are voluntary and can therefore be changed with my help and the family's cooperation.

When I first started out as a family therapist, parents did not expect to come to sessions with their child. But in the past few years, I have noticed that they don't challenge me as much as they used to when I ask them to participate in their child's therapy. They seem to understand that their spousal relationship may be affecting their child. I think we are undergoing a cultural shift. There seems to be a growing awareness, among social and behavioral scientists too, that interpersonal relationships affect children and give rise to their problems in ways that are not always easily understood.

Neuroscientists are actively studying this idea. Daniel Siegel and his colleagues have pioneered a revolutionary new science of interpersonal neurobiology, which maintains that relationships in a child's family affect the neural circuits of the child's brain. According to these scientists, the brain does not contain a hardwired genetic plan that determines our lives. Rather, it is an exquisitely social organ with the capacity to rewire itself in response to changing events and relationships. Neurobiology's growing awareness of the brain's plasticity—its power to change—is especially hopeful. It allows us to see children's problems not as genetically or biologically determined "disorders" but rather as responses to relationships in their lives that can be altered with family therapy.

One of the principles of family therapy is that when a child's parents have a strong relationship and build clear boundaries around themselves as a couple, the child tends to do well. But if the parents don't work out their issues with each other privately, then the child is likely to take sides with one of the parents. These alliances, as we will see in the next chapter, can give rise to serious trouble.

FIVE

Invisible Alliances

WHEN I WAS A CHILD, I sometimes saw monsters in the dark as I was falling asleep at night. These were of course shadows in shapes that my childish imagination could construe as scary monsters. To feel safe, I would pull the covers over my head and close my eyes. Then I was able to drift off to sleep. In the morning the monsters were gone and I didn't give them a second thought. It never occurred to me to wonder if they were real or not, any more than a child who has an imaginary friend asks herself if the friend is real. Children believe in many kinds of imaginary beings that they know are not exactly real yet exist for them in some way or other. Unlike adults, children don't always distinguish sharply between reality and nonreality. And therapists who work with children must keep in mind this difference between adults and children.

...   .

One day last autumn, a very worried mother called me about an unusual problem that her daughter was having. "My daughter feels like invisible people are watching her. She's very frightened," Alice Farnsworth said in a faltering voice on the phone. She continued, "My sister-in-law is a nurse and she thought that Katelyn might be having delusions or hallucinations. She said Katelyn could have schizophrenia or paranoia. Do you work with this kind of problem in children?"

I tried to be reassuring, as Alice's high-pitched voice sounded tense and worried. "Yes, I do. I've treated children with all kinds of fears," I told her, sidestepping the diagnostic question of schizophrenia or paranoia. In fact, although I see children with a range of anxieties, the fear of being watched by "invisible people" is something I'd seen only twice before. "How old is Katelyn?" I asked Alice.

"She just turned ten."

"Why don't you and your husband bring Katelyn in later this week?" I checked my schedule. "How about Thursday at, say, four o'clock?"

"Thank-you, we'll be there," Alice said.

Thursday was a perfect autumn day. The air was crisp and the sky was a deep robin's egg blue. I was excited about meeting Katelyn and her family. The case was especially intriguing to me, not just because "feeling watched by invisible people" is unusual but also because of the difference between adults and children in regard to this symptom.

If an adult reported that he or she felt watched by invisible people, a therapist might well regard it as a delusion. In psychiatry, a delusion is a fixed belief that is resistant to reason, such as a man's claim that he is Jesus Christ or the king of England. This would be a sign of a serious disorder for which medication might be a viable option. A hallucination is a perception of something that does not exist outside the mind. The ghost of Hamlet's father, for example, is sometimes played as a hallucination. The hallucinations associated with schizophrenia, however, are typically auditory—usually described as "hearing voices"—rather than visual.

One must be cautious when thinking about delusions or even hallucinations with children, for children are very different from adults in how they experience the world. Children have a rich fantasy life, where make-believe and everyday reality frequently intersect. The pediatrician and child psychiatrist Donald Winnicott calls the imaginative world of children a "play space." This is where Santa Claus, Winnie the Pooh, and the tooth fairy exist. Winnicott emphasizes that adults should not challenge a child's imaginative beliefs in the same way we would challenge adults who held the same beliefs. We wouldn't think of telling a young boy that the tooth fairy is a figment of his imagination, but we would certainly have concerns if his mother expected a winged creature to bestow a gift on her when she lost a tooth.

I had these ideas in mind as I anticipated the Farnsworth family's visit. When I walked into the waiting room at 4:00 p.m., Katelyn was reading the latest issue of *National Geographic Kids*. She was very pretty, with pale skin, high cheekbones, and blond hair pulled back in a ponytail. Her parents, Warren and Alice, were having a quiet conversation in which they seemed to be disagreeing about something. They were both tall with blond hair and blue eyes. Alice wore an elegant white linen dress. I greeted them and shook hands, and we walked into my office.

Alice spoke first. "Katelyn feels like she's being watched by invisible people."

"Really?" I asked, turning to Katelyn. "So you don't actually see them, but you feel like they are there watching you?"

"Yes. And it's scary."

"And how often do you feel like the people are watching you? Is it every day, twice a day, or more often?" I wanted to get a baseline for the frequency of Katelyn's experience, so that I would be able to tell when we were seeing improvement.

"It's almost all the time," Katelyn replied. I was surprised that she didn't have any hesitancy about talking to me. She seemed like an exceptionally verbal and outgoing child, and her vocabulary was sophisticated for a ten-year-old. I thought to myself that her parents probably had conversations with her about a variety of topics, and undoubtedly encouraged her to read books beyond her grade level. "And the invisible people make you feel scared?"

"I feel *really* scared. Sometimes I get scared at night and then I run into Mommy and Daddy's room."

"Katelyn has been sleeping in our bed lately. It seems to comfort her," Warren said.

"But it's not a permanent solution," Alice added. Warren nodded in agreement, frowning as if to say that they had tolerated this behavior long enough.

"What makes you scared at night?" I asked Katelyn.

"I'm afraid that Mommy or Daddy will die. My friend's mother died in a car accident."

Alice clarified: "This happened a few months ago. It was really tragic. She had three children."

"I see. That was very sad." So Katelyn's fear was somewhat reality based. I asked her, "Do the invisible people ever talk to you?"

"No!" Katelyn said emphatically, as though my question were silly. "They just watch me."

Now that I had a better understanding of Katelyn's experience, I needed to hear a little more about the family. Katelyn was looking hopefully in the direction of the sand tray and miniatures, so I invited her to play while I talked with her parents. I told her that she was welcome to join our conversation at any time. Katelyn didn't need any more prompting. She went over to the sand tray, sat down next to it, and started picking out tiny figurines and examining them.

"Look, Mom. Here's Dorothy, and the green witch, and the Munchkins."

"We took her to see *Wicked* for her birthday, so she's really into *Wizard of Oz,*" Warren explained.

"Is Katelyn having any problems at school?" I asked, shifting the conversation to the matter at hand.

"No, she's not really having problems as such," said Alice. "But her teacher told us at the last parent-teacher conference that she wasn't working up to her full potential. We agree with that."

Alice and Warren told me they had two boys, ages fourteen and sixteen, Warren's sons from his first marriage. Warren had full custody and the boys lived with them. "I think it's hard for her because her brothers are so much older than she is. Sometimes I think she feels left out," said Alice. I looked over at Katelyn, but she was engrossed in her sand play. I asked about the parents' jobs. Warren was a high school drama and music teacher, and Alice was a project manager at an electronics company. Our time was almost up. Katelyn, meanwhile, had filled the sand tray with patterns of shells, leaves, and figurines. The arrangements were strikingly colorful and varied. What a rich imagination this girl has, I thought to myself.

I took out one of my little notebooks and said to Katelyn, "I'd like you to write in this notebook every time you feel the invisible people watching you. Write the day and the exact time that it happens. Then write about all the feelings you're having. Write about everything you're thinking and whatever you feel. Don't leave anything out. That's very important. Write down every detail. Okay?"

"Okay," Katelyn said, taking the notebook.

"And I'd like to talk with Katelyn alone next week." We made an appointment, and they left.

As I prepared myself for the session with Katelyn, I had several questions in mind. Who was her symptom protecting—perhaps her mother, or was it someone else? Usually a symptom has a specific function in the family. Was Katelyn drawing attention to herself in a very dramatic way to distract her parents from some problem of their own? What was the metaphorical meaning of the invisible people?

I opted to frame Katelyn's unusual symptom just as I would approach any other childhood fear. I did not choose to see it as a delusion, any more than I would think that a child who told me that she had an invisible friend or saw monsters in the dark was delusional.

I decided that a strategic dialogue would help Katelyn feel better and help me uncover more about the meaning of the invisible people. This is the technique I used with Elizabeth, in which I asked her a series of carefully designed questions about precisely how she washed her hands—with hot water or cold, with soap or without soap. By using this dialogue, I had let Elizabeth know that I fully accepted her hand washing and wanted to understand more about her experience. With Katelyn, I was hoping to find exceptions or times when she didn't feel she was being watched or when she felt less scared. Hitting upon these exceptions in the strategic dialogue actually gives the child the feeling of being more in control of her fears or other problem behavior such as hand washing. The strategic dialogue addresses the child at the level of perception and feeling, not merely at the level of thinking.

At our next visit, Katelyn came in willingly and sat down on the couch. We looked through her worry book together. She had dutifully made an entry at least once a day, writing that people were watching her and that she felt scared. She also wrote about a mean girl at school who was trying to take a friend away from her. Katelyn seemed comfortable talking with me, so I decided it was time for my invariant question.

"Are you more worried about your mother or your father?" I asked. She replied right away, "I'm more worried about my mother. When she comes home from work, she screams at everyone because she's really stressed out."

"Is she stressed out about her job?"

"Yes, I think mostly it's her job. But she also fights with my father. He's not that nice to her. Like once Daddy yelled at Mommy that he was sick and tired of her asking him to fix things around the house. Then Mommy went into the bedroom and slammed the door really hard. That was scary." For a ten-year-old, Katelyn certainly had more than her share of worries. I would have to talk with her parents about this. I jotted down a few notes and then turned to the strategic dialogue.

"Do you recognize the invisible people, or are they strangers?" I asked. Katelyn thought about this for a few moments. Then she said that the faces of the invisible people seemed to be familiar, like the faces of some of the kids at school. Good, I thought to myself. She was choosing the less scary alternative. My goal was to have her experience the feeling as less frightening.

"Do you feel like the people are going to hurt you, or are they just watching you?"

"No, I don't feel like they're going to hurt me. They just watch me." Again she picked the more benign alternative. Of course, I didn't pursue this line of questioning because I didn't want her to think the experience was scarier than it actually was. In the strategic dialogue, the child typically chooses the less frightening of the alternatives, thus moving gently toward a reframing of her experience. So Katelyn's invisible people turned out to be known to her, not strangers, and harmless instead of harmful.

At each step, Katelyn chose the more benign alternative, so that slowly she began to feel that there was nothing really threatening about the situation. Now it was time to paraphrase what Katelyn had told me. Paraphrasing makes the child feel in charge of the conversation, as though she is leading the way and I am just trying to follow her train of thought. Many children's symptoms serve the purpose of giving the child a feeling of control in a difficult situation. Having a symptom, especially a worrisome symptom, gets a lot of parental attention that the child might feel she cannot get in any other way. The symptom thus becomes a child's attempted way of gaining more attention from her parents. But this solution itself becomes a problem in which the child eventually feels trapped. The strategic dialogue offers her a way out. The more sense of control I could give Katelyn, the less trapped she would feel.

"So you feel that the people watching you are familiar people, kind of like the kids at school. And they don't mean you any harm. Is that right? Do I understand you correctly?" I was putting her in charge by making her the expert on her own problem. And in making her the expert, in a sense I was putting myself "one down."

"Yes," said Katelyn. "That's right."

"Okay. Good. Do you have this feeling more often when you're alone or when you're with other people?" She thought about this for a minute.

"It's more when I'm alone, like after my dad drops me off at home after school. When I'm on a playdate or at the park with my friends, I don't feel like the people are watching me."

I had now found an exception. There was less of a problem when Katelyn was with friends, more so when she was alone—especially when her dad dropped her off. Was she feeling cut off from her father? I was now forming a hunch, a working hypothesis.

I said to Katelyn, "Maybe you're just feeling lonely." At these words, Katelyn breathed an audible sigh of relief and sank back into the couch cushions. Her face relaxed. She clearly felt that now I understood her. Katelyn told me that she did feel lonely, especially in the afternoons. Her brothers usually had basketball practice or games, so often there was nobody at home with her. Even if her brothers didn't have practice, they played basketball in the backyard and ignored her. She felt left out.

I told her that I would speak with her parents about this. Perhaps sometimes they could arrange for her to be at a friend's house after school. Or maybe her father could spend a little time with her. Katelyn also told me that occasionally she felt pressured by her mother to do things perfectly, especially her schoolwork. She loved to work with her mother on art projects, but her mother was critical—every little thing had to be perfect. Ah, I thought to myself. A critical parent might well make a child feel like she was being watched.

Alice came to the next session without Warren, who had to fly to Sacramento to visit his mother in the hospital. I asked how Katelyn was doing, and Alice told me that her feeling of being watched was "a little bit less often." I was happy to hear that. I have noticed many times that the strategic dialogue can bring about a change in a child's feelings and perceptions even after a single session. Also, I was happy that her mother was seeing improvement. This would give her confidence in me and make it more likely that she and her husband would comply with my directives.

I asked Alice if she and Warren had arguments in front of the children. Alice told me that she sometimes felt undermined by Warren when she tried to discipline the children, and his attitude made her angry. She said that he always wanted to be the good guy, a buddy to the kids, which forced her to be the bad guy, the disciplinarian. Alice candidly told me that she felt like their family was split into "two warring tribes." Warren and his sons were in one tribe, and she and Katelyn were in the other. If she said that one of the boys had to do a chore or walk the dogs, Warren would object that the boy had too much homework. If she asked Warren to fix the garbage disposal, he would think of a million reasons why he couldn't get to it that day. And then he'd forget about it entirely. Instead of spending time together in the evenings, Warren would retreat to his study and play video games. "I wish that just once he would suggest watching a movie together or going out to dinner. I wish he would come over and hold my hand," Alice said. "I feel like I'm staying in this marriage only for the children."

Alice described Katelyn as the "mom defender," the one who always sided with her. I could well imagine that Katelyn was bearing the brunt of all this family strife. Not surprisingly, the most vulnerable member of the family had become symptomatic of more deep-seated problems between the parents. At first glance, at least, the child who is the most empathic and caring becomes the "identified patient," the one with the problem. But in truth the family is the patient. Anyone in the family can be the identified patient; it is not always a child. A husband can become depressed. A wife can become agoraphobic or have panic attacks. A young adult can drop out of college and start to use drugs. But in all these situations we must look at the purpose or function that the symptom is serving in the family. Who is becoming more connected by the symptom? For what larger problem is the symptom a distraction?

Alice's narrative made the source of Katelyn's problems clearer to me. Instead of the parents maintaining a healthy hierarchy, with clear boundaries around them, Katelyn's father was allied with his sons and cutting Katelyn's mother off emotionally. This pushed the mother and daughter toward "enmeshment," or overcloseness, their mutual loneliness driving them together. I could imagine that Katelyn's loneliness was a reflection of her mother's loneliness in her marriage. Warren had distanced himself because of his wife's demands and expectations of him. Alice and Warren's situation reminded me of what famed family therapist Salvador Minuchin calls the "signature arrangement of the troubled middle-class family." A mother's closeness to one of her children is an emotional substitute for intimacy in her marriage. A father, too, can substitute closeness with a child for closeness with his wife. No wonder Katelyn had become symptomatic.

But Katelyn's particular symptom was not inevitable. The reason the symptom took the particular form it did might have had something to do with her feeling scrutinized by her mother and held accountable for any little mistake. A family therapist cannot know precisely why a child has one symptom and not another, or why one child in a family takes on the role of the identified patient, leaving the other children to go about their normal lives. And then again, many marriages come to the brink of divorce without a child having symptoms at all. No matter how well family therapists understand family dynamics, some puzzles always remain.

Alice didn't wear her emotional vulnerability on her sleeve. She had the outward persona of a tough, competent, and intelligent woman who seemed very much in charge of any situation. But beneath her strong outward demeanor I could see that she was also angry—and lonely. An old Irish proverb says "Strife is better than loneliness." Couples who are lonely in their marriage often fight because the anger gives them at least some trace of connectedness with each other. Fighting may be an attempt to restore their lost connection, and can be a substitute for lost intimacy.

Alice revealed another cross-generational alliance that could possibly spell trouble. Warren's mother had lived with them for the year following her divorce. This was eight years ago. Alice felt that her mother-in-law had always taken her husband's side about discipline and was the source of many conflicts between the couple. She ignored Alice's rule that the boys had to be in their rooms by 9:30 on school nights—sometimes watching television with them until 10:30 or 11:00 p.m. Finally, Alice had insisted to Warren that either her mother-in-law move out or she would move out. Warren eventually did ask his mother to leave. Alice had tears in her eyes as she told me the story. Since this incident, she had built up an emotional wall between herself and her husband. But for all she had been through or perhaps because of it, Alice had remained strong. I admired her devotion to her children and her determination to help her daughter, however painful the journey might be.

Toward the end of the session, I mentioned that Katelyn had told me she felt lonely at home after school. Could Alice pay one of

Katelyn's brothers to babysit for her? Alice thought that was a good idea—the boys always needed money. "But they'd have to play a game with her or take her out somewhere to earn the money," she said. I thought that would help a lot. Katelyn would love the attention from her brothers. I also asked if Warren could spend a little time with Katelyn after school. A general rule, when trying to strengthen boundaries around parents, is to get the less involved parent more involved with the symptomatic child. Alice questioned this, as I thought she might. But in the end I convinced her, and Warren made time in his day to do this.

I then scheduled an appointment for Katelyn and a separate session for Alice and Warren. And I wrote out a few simple recommendations for the parents—to keep their arguments away from the children, to pay their sons to babysit Katelyn, to go out together on a date once a week, and to avoid putting too much pressure on Katelyn. I suggested that Warren be the one to help Katelyn with her homework. I also suggested that Alice try to go to the gym to relieve her stress. I asked that both parents make a point of reassuring Katelyn that they were taking good care of their health to try to allay her fears about their dying.

Alice asked me, in her typical direct fashion, what all these written recommendations were meant to accomplish. Jay Haley used to say that family therapists should not share their views about the protective function of a child's symptom with parents. I tend to follow his advice and keep my reasoning to myself. But since Alice did ask, as parents sometimes do, I felt I owed her a straightforward answer. I told her that I thought that Katelyn was protecting her with her symptom by deflecting Alice's attention from the other stresses in her life and the marital discord. Alice understood this very well. "I was the protector in my own family," she told me. She said that it would take her and her husband a little time to implement my strategies, but she understood the rationale behind them.

At her session two weeks later, Katelyn told me that her feeling of being watched was "less often." From feeling it all the time, she said she now felt it "about three times a day," and the feeling wasn't as scary.

"It feels more normal now," she told me. "It almost feels like I'm an actress on a stage and an audience is watching me."

I thought to myself that her parents must be implementing my directives thoroughly to be seeing this much improvement in so short a time. I asked Katelyn how her parents were, and she told me that her mother wasn't yelling as much. Katelyn wasn't worried about her mother anymore and no longer feared her parents dying. Good, I thought. Therapy was helping.

I asked Katelyn if she was still writing about her fears in her worry notebook. She told me that she "was getting lazy" about writing. This is typical. Although the notebook helps at first, when the child starts to feel better she tends to forget to write about her problem. The worry notebook is a strategy that parents can easily use with their children, even without therapy. Journals and diaries have long been a method of externalizing unpleasant feelings and reducing their intensity. Just writing down their concerns often makes children feel better, whether or not they discuss their worries with an adult.

Katelyn told me that her father was spending time at home with her after he picked her up from school. He had started going in to work early so he could stay at home with her after school three days a week. Her brothers seemed to be home more often as well, and they had played Monopoly with her twice. She didn't have much more to talk about in the session, so we played the game of Othello. Katelyn caught on to the game right away, figuring out that she had to secure the corners and the edges of the board. She had never played Othello before, although her father had showed her how to play Reversi, a similar game, on his computer. Katelyn and I had fun discussing strategies.

Old-fashioned board games are a treat for children these days, as they provide the opportunity for personal interaction that computer games and game machines often do not. Sadly, electronic games and the computer itself have supplanted board games and card playing in many families, taking away the intimate contact with parents that these diversions provide. Game playing is a wonderful way for parents and kids to laugh together, strategize together, and engage in healthy competition.

As we've seen, families have a great capacity to heal their members. Katelyn's fear of being watched by invisible people, although it seemed like a terrible problem—one that some therapists might have diagnosed as paranoia—was overcome mainly through the efforts of her parents. The underinvolved parent, in this case her father, began spending more time with Katelyn. My strategic dialogue helped Katelyn, too, by validating her fears and feelings and leading her to reframe her experience as benevolent instead of frightening. She was able to connect the "invisible people" with her ordinary loneliness, and realize that in situations with other people, she did not feel lonely or feel she was being watched.

As much as the strategic dialogue helped Katelyn, I have found that in order to defeat a problem permanently, change also has to occur within the family. Individual techniques, though they are good supplements, by themselves are not enough. A child may feel better after a session of strategic dialogue, or after a session of play therapy for that matter, but if she returns home to an atmosphere of parental hostility or distance, her good feelings will not last very long.

The fourth session, two weeks after I met with Katelyn, was with Alice and Warren. We still had the problem of improving Katelyn's school performance. And I needed to strengthen the parents' marriage so that Katelyn could become a little more disengaged from her mother. At the beginning of the session, Katelyn's parents told me that she showed significant improvement. She was no longer complaining of being watched by invisible people, and she wasn't waking up frightened in the middle of the night and coming into their bed.

Warren and Alice admitted that they were not usually on the same page about discipline. Alice tended to lose patience and yell, while Warren was more easygoing and patient. And, like most parents, Warren and Alice hadn't been aware that their disagreements and negativity might be affecting their child. I suggested some compromises. If Alice backed off on discipline, Warren agreed to take more of a role. He would see to it that the boys did the chores they were supposed to do to earn their allowance.

Then I asked Warren what he needed from Alice. He had plenty of grievances. "No more of your 'to-do' lists," he said. "I have enough on my plate with work and picking up the kids after school. I don't need to come home to lists of things that I'm supposed to do around the house."

"So how are they supposed to get done?" Alice asked angrily. "You won't let me hire a handyman, and you won't do them yourself. The bathroom faucet has been leaking for a year, and you won't call a plumber. The garbage disposal doesn't work. What am I supposed to do?"

"I told you I'll get to them," Warren said.

"But you don't. You never get to them."

This was a problem I had heard many times before. Fortunately I had a useful strategy.

"Warren, I think it might help if you give Alice a time frame for fixing things. Perhaps you could say, 'I don't have time today, but I'll get it fixed by Sunday at seven. If I don't get it done by then, I'll call the plumber on Monday.'"

Warren looked relieved.

"That's a good idea. I like that. As long as I don't feel like I have to fix something right away, I don't mind providing a time frame."

I turned to Alice and asked if that was acceptable to her. She said it was.

It is the little things that wear down a marriage and form the bricks and mortar of the emotional walls between husbands and wives. It's the caps on the toothpaste, the honey-do lists, and the retreats into cyberspace to avoid facing what Virginia Woolf famously called the "dailyness of life." In today's couples, it is not only the wife who faces the second shift of caring for the children and the house after she comes home from a full day of work. Fathers too—at least those in two-income families—come home to a second shift. They make dinner, pick the kids up from baseball practice, coach their teams, and plan playdates. They also help with homework in a world where, unbelievably, kindergarteners can have an hour of homework each day and middle-school children can have up to three hours. Often, too, both parents turn to their own work after the kids are in bed. It's no surprise that this high-pressure home life can lead to disappointments and disagreements that quickly morph into an emotional barrier between parents.

Once the wall is up, breaking it down or even finding a chink in it poses a formidable challenge to the therapist. For me, the critical factor is making sure that both spouses feel that each can be influenced by the other's needs. Husbands and wives must see for themselves that their spouse is willing to modify their own behavior. Even if asking Warren to fix the faucet doesn't seem like a big deal to Alice, the way she asks him to do it may seem like a big deal to him. Giving her husband a wider time frame, instead of asking him to do a task right away, went a long way toward salvaging Alice's and Warren's relationship. Because Warren felt that Alice's job was superior in status to his own (she earned more money than he did), he was especially sensitive to the way she asked him to do tasks around the house.

I have observed that some men think their wives expect them to do what they ask *immediately*. All it takes is an idle comment at dinner like "Y'know, those roses need some cutting back" for these men to think that they are supposed to jump up from the dinner table and put on their gardening gloves. Even if their wives didn't mean they should get to the task anytime soon, the feeling that their wives expect them to do something right away makes these men dig in their heels.

Warren and Alice said that going out alone on a date once a week was also helping them. At least they had time to have a grown-up conversation without the children distracting them every minute. They were hoping to get away by themselves for a week in the summer when the children were at camp. In my experience, a romantic vacation, away from the stresses of work and children, can do wonders to rejuvenate a marriage. It provides an opportunity for intimacy, which is so often lost in a modern marriage because the demands of work, children, and the ever-increasing complexities of modern life seem more pressing than the need for emotional closeness.

Alice admitted that she had probably been putting too much pressure on Katelyn to do well at school. "I'm a perfectionist with myself and everyone around me," she said. Warren seconded that, and encouraged her to lessen the pressure on Katelyn. Alice assured me she would try to ease up on her expectations. We made up a list of Katelyn's good qualities—she was intelligent, a good friend, helpful around the house, fun to be with, and creative—and I asked the parents to sprinkle these compliments into their conversations with Katelyn to enhance her self-esteem. They added the list of positive qualities to the other strategies I had given them.

Then I asked if Katelyn had friends at school. "Her teacher says that there are a few nice girls she's friendly with," Alice said. "But for some reason Katelyn doesn't feel like she has friends. She tells me that she feels like she's left out of the cliques of the popular kids." Perhaps feeling left out at school was a remnant of Katelyn's feeling of being left out by her brothers at home. We talked about planning more play-dates for Katelyn. Warren and Alice were continuing to implement the recommendations I had written down for them. At least they had to have conversations with each other about dealing with Katelyn, which was better than their fighting.

At the final session, Katelyn no longer had feelings of being watched, and didn't feel lonely in the afternoons. I told Warren and Alice that Katelyn no longer needed therapy, but I asked for a telephone update in two months. At that time, they reported that Katelyn was doing fine.

When I first learned about the strategic dialogue as a therapy technique, I didn't feel comfortable with the idea of using it with children. It had been developed for use with adults and has a quasi-hypnotic aspect to it. And, more important, as a family systems therapist, I was accustomed to resolving children's problems by strategic-systemic techniques. I gave parents directives and reorganized families to put parents in charge of their children. I strengthened parental boundaries and sliced through enmeshed parent-child relationships by prescribing date nights and romantic weekend getaways for parents. I told parents to maintain their privacy by locking their bedroom door. I provided parents with ways to help their children soothe themselves—with music and story CDs or tapes—in order to free the marital bed from children. After abandoning play therapy many years ago and falling in love with systemic thinking, I felt resistant to any method of therapy that addressed the individual child instead of the family system.

But since I found the strategic dialogue so effective with older adolescents who were experiencing fears, anxieties, and compulsive behaviors, I thought that there was good reason to try this technique with younger children as well. I approached it cautiously, writing out scripts ahead of time. Today it is one of my most valuable interventions. It is a very gentle strategy, seemingly simple on the surface but actually complex. The questions are not aimless. As in the ancient Socratic dialogues, or the hypnotic techniques of Milton Erickson, the questioner has a final goal in mind and carefully sculpts her questions to reach that goal. By giving an illusion of alternatives, the questioner creates a new feeling right in the session that will be the beginning of a change in the child's perceptions of herself and her world. So when I asked Katelyn if she felt like the invisible people just watched her or if they threatened to hurt her, I was hoping she would choose the less threatening alternative and begin to feel less frightened.

Parents who have observed me using the strategic dialogue are impressed with how it seems to help their child feel better, and they have asked me if they can use the technique themselves. After giving this question careful thought, I came to the conclusion that it probably wouldn't work. The sequence of questions can be difficult to invent and must be tailor-made to the child's individual problem. Creating the questions and asking them in a way that will bring about change is a subtle and complex art. I had to practice the strategic dialogue for more than a year before I got the hang of it. Of course, parents can take a lesson from the "paraphrasing" part of the strategic dialogue. They can listen carefully to what their child tells them and reflect back the child's feelings, which in itself can help a child feel heard and understood.

Loneliness was a central theme in Katelyn's family, and in many ways loneliness is one of the deepest problems of modern life. Mother Teresa once said that loneliness is the greatest impoverishment of a society. Family members are often estranged from one another either by geographical distance or because they cling to old resentments and grudges and don't create opportunities to talk things over. Parents are busy with work and long commutes and have barely enough time to help their children with homework, let alone spend quality time with each other to keep their relationship alive.

Estrangement and loneliness played a central part in the story of fifteen-year-old Margaret, who had received the terrible diagnosis of paranoid schizophrenia before I met her and her family. This case actually began for me with Margaret's ten-year-old sister, Susan, whose teacher had suggested family therapy.

Susan's mother, Josie, called me to make an appointment and asked if she and her husband, Enrique, could come in and meet me first. I told her that would be fine, and I made an appointment for them the following week.

"What can I do for you?" I asked them after we made our introductions. Enrique was a large man, tall and broad shouldered. He worked as a repairman for the telephone company. Enrique's parents had moved to this country from El Salvador. Josie was petite with pale blue eyes. She worked part-time as a librarian.

Josie began. "Our daughter Susan—she's ten—has been crying at school every day. Her teacher has tried hugs and encouragement, but nothing seems to help Susan feel better. The teacher is really worried, and that's why she recommended we see you."

"When did Susan start crying at school?"

"Her teacher said . . ." Josie seemed on the verge of tears herself. "She said she's been crying at school for the past two years. She doesn't cry all the time, just off and on. All of her teachers have told us about it at parent-teacher conferences. They've all been really nice to her, but nothing helps for long." How unusual, I thought. I wonder what is so terrible in this little girl's life to make her cry at school. It must be embarrassing for her to cry in front of her friends.

"And do you know why Susan has been crying? What does she say about it?"

"She started crying when her sister, Margaret, hit her and chased her into her room," said Josie. "It happened a few times. That was about two years ago. Susan told us that Margaret said to her, 'I'm going to kill you!' I'm sure Susan was terrified—she was only eight at the time."

"The teacher told us that when Susan is assigned to write stories in class, she always writes about Margaret," Enrique said in a somber tone.

Josie continued. "We took Margaret to a psychiatrist. He saw her a few times and diagnosed her with paranoid schizophrenia. He recommended medication and therapy. But we thought that was too strong a diagnosis. I asked my friend who's a social worker. She knows Margaret well, and she agreed the diagnosis was not right. Margaret was not having delusions or hearing voices. The only symptom she had was that she was angry and hit her sister."

"So what did you do about the violence?" I asked.

"We never leave the girls alone together in the house," Enrique said. "And I put a lock on Susan's door so she would feel safe in her room. Margaret hasn't hurt Susan again, but she isn't exactly nice to her either."

Margaret certainly has gotten her parent's attention with her violent behavior, I said to myself. Her family seems to be organizing itself around her violence and the need to keep Susan safe.

"So why is Susan still crying at school?" I asked.

"She says she doesn't know why she's so sad," Josie said.

This is an interesting puzzle, I thought. Was Margaret's violence perhaps a metaphor for anger between Enrique and Josie? Or was there some other volatile situation, maybe in the extended family? Was it just sibling rivalry? In order to make sense of the story of Susan crying at school, I needed more information. I asked Josie and Enrique what else had occurred in the family at around the time Margaret's violence began.

They thought about my question and quickly realized that just before Margaret threatened Susan, they had moved into a house on the same street as Enrique's sister and her family. Susan and Margaret affectionately called his sister Auntie Jaycee—her real name was Jocelyn—and the girls were really happy to be living close to their cousins. That first Christmas, Auntie Jaycee invited their family to her house. But instead they had gone to Josie's parents for the holiday. Auntie Jaycee had taken great offense at this, and Enrique's father had also felt insulted. Since that Christmas, Enrique's father had barely spoken to Enrique and had pretty much ignored the girls.

Enrique admitted that he was very hurt that his father ignored his daughters. His father would visit his sister's children down the block but wouldn't even stop in at Enrique's house. And his sister wouldn't allow her children to see Susan and Margaret.

"Is there anything you can do to reconcile with your father?" I asked. I could imagine how hurtful this situation was to the girls.

"We've tried," said Josie, "but Enrique's father is a proud and stubborn man. Once he is offended, he doesn't forget it easily."

I decided to put aside for the moment the situation with the grandfather and aunt and focus on getting the parents in charge of Margaret's behavior. Right now, the threat of Margaret's becoming violent was controlling the family. Josie and Enrique were always on the alert, afraid that the terrible diagnosis Margaret had received was true and that violence could erupt at any time. I decided to frame Margaret's hitting her sister as a behavior problem instead of viewing it as a frightening psychiatric disorder and gave her parents some strategies.

I told the parents to clearly state to Margaret the rules she had to follow with respect to Susan. She was not to yell at her, hit her, or in any way threaten her. If she did, she would have to do a half-hour "helping chore," supervised by her father. If she refused to do the chore, she would lose her cell phone and not get her allowance that week. Together, we made a list of chores that Margaret could do around the house. In addition to a chore for being mean to her sister, Margaret would have to buy Susan a gift from her own allowance.

To address Susan's sadness until I could intervene with the family, I asked the parents to see to it that Susan laughed every day. Josie was to take Susan to the library and check out books of cartoons and humor. They were to read these every evening. In the morning, they should read the comics in the newspaper together. I chose not to label Susan's crying as depression, reframing it instead as sadness. The simple strategy of bringing laughter into a child's life can be very effective for the whole family. Laughter, scientists tell us, stimulates endorphins in the brain that produce a feeling of well-being. Of course if a child seems sad for a prolonged length of time and for no apparent reason, parents should consult a family therapist.

I was guessing that Susan's sadness and her sister's violence were connected to the situation between her parents and her aunt and grandfather. As we saw with Cindy's family in Chapter 4, a child's troubled behavior can stem not only from a conflict between her parents; it can also be rooted in a conflict involving a grandparent. I asked Josie and Enrique to bring the girls to the next session, and we found a time that was convenient for everyone.

When I greeted the family in the waiting room on the day of the appointment, Margaret hung back, thumbing through a magazine and seeming reluctant to come into my office. In a few minutes she joined us. I started out by introducing myself to the girls and telling them that I had met once with their parents. Then I asked Josie and Enrique to explain why they were here.

"We want Susan to be happier," Josie said.

Margaret started to tap the floor with her toe.

"Could you please ask Margaret to stop the tapping? It's disruptive," I said to Enrique.

"Margaret, cut it out," Enrique said. Margaret glared at me but stopped tapping her foot.

When I raised the subject of Aunt Jaycee and the girl's grandfather, the girls had a lot to say.

"They are being hateful to us," Margaret said angrily. "And it's especially hurtful to my dad." Turning to her father, she said, "You can't trust Grandpa. He's done this before. You get close and then he gets cold and distant. I never want to see him again."

"She's right," Susan said, speaking for the first time. "You can't trust Grandpa, Dad. It's not worth trying." I could see that the girls were being protective of their father. Usually violence in children is a sign of parental discord. But it can also signify discord between parents and grandparents. Was Margaret's violence a way to focus her father's attention away from the breach with his own father, and was it at the same time a metaphor for the emotional violence of the rift?

Over the next few weeks, Margaret's behavior improved. Her father was monitoring her behavior toward her sister, and Margaret had had to do only two chores. Susan was starting to feel better. With her parents' permission, I spoke to Susan's teacher, who said that Susan was not crying at school lately and seemed a little more cheerful. The teacher felt that Susan had been crying because she seemed to be carrying the burden of her family's troubles—and the burden was too much for her. The teacher of course didn't know all the details, except for scraps of information that Susan had disclosed in her writing assignments. The teacher was pleased to hear that Susan's family was in counseling.

Somehow the grandfather heard about the girls' problems, and he had written to Margaret, sending her a gift of money for her sixteenth birthday, which took place a month after the family started therapy. At the next session, Margaret brought me a copy of the letter she had written to her grandfather. She trusted me now, since she saw that I wanted to help her father. In the letter, she wrote that she never thought of him as her grandfather because he didn't want to have anything to do with her family. She accused him of always giving her cousins gifts and taking them places on their birthday, while ignoring her and Susan. Most of all, she accused him of ignoring her father on his birthday, hurting not only her and her sister but also their father. She ended the letter with the question, "What have we ever done to you to make you treat us so cruelly?"

I sympathized with Margaret. Now I understood that she was protecting her father from her grandfather. This is not as common as a child protecting a parent, but it does occur. I told Margaret that she and Susan should focus on school and their activities, and let me take on the job of healing the rift in their family.

Margaret looked at me skeptically. "Can you do that? Can you talk to my grandfather?"

"Absolutely," I told her, hoping I sounded confident. The truth was that I had no idea if I would be able to get her grandfather into a session. But I was going to try. If nothing else, I would be able to talk with the grandfather on the phone or write him a letter.

Although Enrique was reluctant to invite his father to a session, I persuaded him that it had to be done for the sake of his daughters. I said that I was sure the girls would continue to have problems if the rift between him and his father was not resolved.

"Why does this have to hurt my kids?" asked Enrique. He had started to cry. "My relationship with my father has nothing to do with them."

Parents ask me questions like this all the time. Like Enrique, most of us think of emotional pain as an individual feeling, for that is how we are used to experiencing it. But to think of pain in one member of a family as simply an individual feeling is to some extent an illusion. From a family systems perspective, the family is an organic whole, and sorrow in one area can pop up somewhere else in the system.

I tried to explain to Enrique that pain and loneliness in a family overflow the boundaries of the individual and can be felt by other family members, especially children. I assured him that this wasn't his fault—he had done nothing wrong. Enrique finally agreed, with great reluctance, to have his father come to a session with him and Josie. We decided the girls should not be present; they didn't need to witness the volatile emotions that were bound to emerge.

Enrique said his father would be more likely to come if I made the call and set up the appointment. But he didn't think his father would come to see a therapist because he was very traditional, and therapy wasn't part of his culture. Although it would be unusual for a psychodynamically oriented therapist to make a phone call to a member of a client's extended family, family therapists do this all the time—especially with families being harmed by long-standing grudges.

In the end, the grandfather did come in. He arrived early for the session. He was a tall, dignified-looking man, with white hair and a white beard. Josie arrived a few minutes later, but there was no sign of Enrique. I was starting to worry that Enrique wasn't going to show up because it would be too painful to see his father. But finally he arrived, looking nervous.

After I introduced myself and shook hands with Enrique's father, Albert, I explained that, for the sake of his granddaughters, the differences between him and his son and daughter-in-law had to be resolved. Enrique explained that the favoritism his father showed to his sister's children was hurtful to his daughters, and he wished his father would treat all the cousins equally. Albert suddenly became furious.

"It's all your fault," he said, his voice rising to a shout as he pointed at Josie. "You kept me from seeing my granddaughters at Christmas two years ago. We were all supposed to be together for Christmas at Jocelyn's house, right after you moved into the neighborhood. You just decided everything and Enrique went along with it."

When Josie tried to defend herself, reminding him that her mother had gotten out of the hospital after her hip replacement just before Christmas, Albert became so angry that his tanned face turned bright red. Abruptly, he got to his feet and walked out of the office, leaving us all shocked. Enrique shook his head, saying that it was useless to try to talk about feelings with his father. Josie turned to me and apologized.

"I was afraid something like this might happen if Albert came. I hope you're not offended."

"Oh, no, of course I'm not offended," I told her. "It's not the first time that someone has stormed out of my office." Hearing the way others feel about you can be painful, and walking away is the ultimate way of defending against the pain. The three of us sat there in silence for two long minutes. Josie started to cry softly. I handed her a box of tissues.

And then, while I was wondering what to do next, an astonishing thing happened. Albert came back into the office, sat down, and apologized to me. Turning to his son and daughter-in-law, he said, "When I die, I will not be able to leave buildings or monuments with my name on them. All I have to leave behind is my grandchildren. So now I'm going to do what I can to help them lead happy lives. The past is the past."

During the rest of the session, I suggested to Albert that he spend roughly equal time between his daughter's children and his son's. I recommended that he try to treat the cousins as equally as possible. I also suggested that Albert ask his daughter, Jocelyn, to become friendlier with Enrique's family. "Your granddaughters really miss their aunt and their cousins," I told him.

After this dramatic session, things began to change. Albert sent Susan a belated birthday present with a friendly note. Enrique visited his father and started calling him once a week. Josie invited Albert for Sunday dinner at their house, and he brought gifts for the girls. Auntie Jaycee was back in their lives again, and the girls visited her house and played with their cousins.

Over the next few years, Margaret did not hit her sister again.

Their relationship became much better, and she would occasionally invite Susan to go to a movie with her. I continued to see the family periodically for three years. One crisis erupted when Enrique injured his head in a fall, suffered a concussion, and had to take disability leave from work. Margaret came to see me, complaining of headaches; her symptom once again was a metaphor for her father's pain. The strategy that helped her was for Enrique to reassure Margaret that his head was healing well and he would soon be back to work. He told her that physical therapy was helping him regain balance and strength. He invited her to come to a physical therapy session with him to see how much progress he was making.

I coached the parents to be positive and hopeful with Margaret, and not to let her overhear any of their financial or other worries. They saw me for several sessions of marriage counseling. Margaret graduated high school with her class, getting an award in English literature. She went on to community college and did well. After the first few weeks of family therapy, Susan did not cry at school anymore.

Grudges and resentments can wreak dreadful damage in families, as they did in Enrique's. And they challenge the family therapist to come up with creative interventions. I framed Susan's crying at school as a metaphor for her family's pain at being cut off from their grandfather, aunt, and cousins. And I saw Margaret's violence not as psychotic behavior but as an effort to protect her father from the pain of his rift with her grandfather and from the grandfather's anger at her mother.

In a fascinating case described by Salvador Minuchin, the repercussions from resentment played a powerful role in creating a girl's symptoms. Eleven-year-old Jill could not move her left leg or arm. Medical tests showed no physiological cause for her paralysis, and Dr. Minuchin decided to treat it as a problem of relationships in the girl's family. Jill's grandfather initiated the therapy, calling Dr. Minuchin at the Philadelphia Child Guidance Clinic.

In the first session, attended by Jill, her mother, and her mother's parents (Jill's father, Richard, was out of town on business), Jill entered the room leaning on her mother and dragging her leg. Minuchin soon uncovered an underground resentment in Jill's parents' marriage. Jill's father was an engineer for an international oil company; a few years earlier, he had been assigned to Caracas, Venezuela, and had moved his family there. Jill's mother, Janet, fiercely resented the move. She had been happy with her career, her friends, and her house in Houston. She had sacrificed all of these for her husband's career.

During the year in Venezuela, Janet's love for her husband drained away bit by bit, poisoned by her anger and resentment at leaving the life she loved for what she felt was a bleak existence in a city she hated. Before long, Janet's reluctance about moving emerged as a symptom in her daughter. At least this was the hypothesis that Minuchin formed while talking with the family during the first session.

Salvador Minuchin was trained as a psychiatrist. But he approached Jill's problem—which Freud would have called "hysterical paralysis"—from an interpersonal perspective. He treated the paralysis not simply by exploring Jill's psychological state but by focusing on the relationships, alliances, and boundaries in her family.

Janet's resentment toward her husband resulted in her withdrawing emotionally from him and becoming closer to her own parents. Just as Janet leaned on her parents, using them as a crutch to move away from her husband, her daughter was using her as a crutch, leaning on her in order to walk. The daughter's symptom was a metaphor both for her mother's reluctance to move to Caracas and her increasing emotional dependence on her own parents. Like Katelyn, Jill became overly allied with her mother in the silent war that her mother was waging against her father.

Minuchin decided to use a three-step plan to guide Jill to autonomy. Step one was to hook up the disengaged parent, Jill's father, with his daughter to help her move away from her mother. The second step was to move Janet closer to her husband: to address the conflicts in their marriage and draw a firmer boundary between Janet and her daughter. The third step was to intervene directly with Jill to explore the meaning of her symptom and challenge her paralysis. A final intervention would be to address Janet's enmeshment with her own parents—who supported her in disengaging from her husband. Minuchin knew that a daughter's enmeshment with her mother usually mirrored the mother's enmeshment with her own mother. Wise parents, who look to the well-being of their grandchildren, respect the boundaries of their son's or daughter's marriage. Janet was not as self-reliant as she might have been, which meant that it was easy for her to drift back toward her own parents when she was unhappy with her husband. And Janet's parents were more than pleased to become overly close with their daughter to fill the void in their own lives.

Minuchin worked on all these levels to help Jill walk again. Not only did he have to restore and rearrange boundaries in her mother's marriage and extended family, he also worked one-on-one with Jill. He sent her to a practitioner who used the Alexander technique—a bodywork system of improving physical and psychological awareness —which helped her release stress and regain movement in her muscles. Another important strategy—one that I use frequently with parents—was to get Jill's parents to go on a three-day trip together, with instructions to Richard to be especially solicitous to his wife. This would help strengthen the boundary around the parents as a couple. Because Janet loved New England, they stayed in a romantic country inn in Vermont, in a room with a fireplace and canopy bed. And they discovered that they liked being alone together. Janet returned from the trip feeling much better about their relationship. She thought she could finally forgive her husband for disrupting her life.

At the end of the month, the family had to return to Caracas.

Although there had been progress, Jill was still using a cane to walk.

In a final session with Minuchin, which occurred six months later—with the family flying to Philadelphia from Caracas to see him—Minuchin asked Jill if she was sometimes afraid that her parents would separate, and Jill admitted that she was. She was worried because they were still arguing and because some of her parents' friends had divorced. Minuchin, an incomparable showman, drew out the hidden meanings of her cane. One minute it was like a security blanket, something on which Jill was dependent. The next minute, Minuchin used the cane to hook Richard's leg and then Janet's, pulling Janet closer to her husband. "It's a parent catcher," announced Minuchin. Having established the metaphor, Minuchin asked Jill if she felt like she needed to "hook" her parents together. After a silence, Jill answered "yes."

Once Jill's fear of her parents divorcing was out in the open, Richard reassured her that their arguing was just a way of discussing issues, which was better than keeping things inside where they could fester and become worse. He told her that their arguments were not a sign that they were going to divorce. Jill pointed out that her parents sometimes called each other mean names. They admitted this but told her it was not a cause for her to worry. Sometimes parents could be childish.

At this point, Minuchin, in his inimitable theatrical way, held up the cane and told Jill's parents that it was also a symbol of Jill's feeling that *they* needed *her*—and her symptom. Then he had them tell Jill that they didn't need her to have a symptom in order for them to stay together. They had no intention of separating. In a final move, Minuchin declared that he would keep the cane and Jill would have to lean on her parents if she needed support. Jill looked at him very seriously but said nothing.

A few weeks later, after the family returned to Caracas, Jill wrote

Minuchin a letter. "I'm finally walking without a cane," she told him. Minuchin was thrilled.

In this exceptionally challenging case, Minuchin had to move back and forth among many levels—the individual, her parents, and the extended family—many times over. He used metaphor to understand the meaning of the symptom and the role it played in Jill's family. He thought in terms of metaphor to arrive at the meaning of the cane as a parent hook. He also used the idea of the protective function of Jill's strange symptom—to keep her parents from separating. Only by fully involving the members of Jill's family and rearranging alliances was Minuchin able to help her walk normally again.

Up to now, most of the parents I have been talking about have been cooperative in therapy, following my recommendations because they trusted that I knew how to help their child. These compliant parents are a joy to work with. But what of those parents who can't— or won't—follow a therapist's recommendations, even to help their children? In these situations, family therapists have to use indirect techniques, which are usually paradoxical. They are paradoxical because the therapist prescribes more of the very behavior that the family has come to therapy to change. I've already described a few paradoxical interventions—prescribing Joey's resistance at bedtime and prescribing more hand washing for Elizabeth. In the next chapter I have more to say about this fascinating and surprisingly effective type of intervention.

SIX

Reading by Not Reading

The Power of Paradox

THERAPISTS OF ALL PERSUASIONS have observed that a surprising number of people come to therapy saying they want to change, but in the course of treatment they are not able to move off the dime. These are the contrarians—the "yes, but" people who always find a way to reject the therapist's suggestions. They're also the "OK I get it" people, who in fact don't get it. People like this often languish for months or even years in individual talk therapy, unable or unwilling to make the changes they claim to want so desperately—whether it's a new job, a new romantic partner, or simply peace of mind. Children, too, can be contrarians. We all know the boy who insists on going to school in February in a T-shirt and shorts, or the girl whose hair hangs over her eyes, to the constant consternation of her mother. But it's the contrarian or resistant parents we are most concerned with in family therapy because it is they who hold the fate of their children in their hands.

Resistant clients—whether they are adults or children—demand a high level of creativity and even cunning on the part of the therapist because direct interventions will not do the job. Even when it comes to their children, some parents simply cannot bring themselves to follow a therapist's directions. A mother may say to me, "I will do anything to help my son." But soon it becomes clear that she is not following my recommendations, sending me the unspoken and contradictory message that "I want you to get rid of my child's worrisome symptoms, but I'm not going to do what you tell me to do." With these parents, I have to arrange the situation so that whether they do what I recommend or rebel against me, their child's problem will be resolved. This is the type of indirect approach that I took with the parents of eight-year-old Samantha.

Samantha's father, Ray, came to therapy first.

"I'm sorry my wife couldn't come today," Ray said when I greeted him in the waiting room. "She's having one of her bad days and didn't feel up to it. I hope it's all right for me to come by myself."

On the phone, Ray had told me that he and his wife wanted to meet me before they brought in their daughter. It's not unusual for parents to want to "interview" a therapist to whom they are entrusting their child's well-being. On my part, I welcome an initial interview session because I need parents to be comfortable so we can work cooperatively to help their child. One of Ray's colleagues had recommended me; I had treated his daughter, who had symptoms similar to Samantha's, without having to refer her to a psychiatrist for medication. Ray and his wife did not want to medicate Samantha if they could avoid it.

"What can I do for you?" I asked after Ray had taken a seat on the couch.

"We're worried about our daughter, Samantha. She just turned eight. She's our only child." There was a pause.

"Yes," I said encouragingly.

"Her teacher says that Samantha has trouble paying attention and focusing. Her grades are falling. She recently got a D on a math test. And the teacher says Samantha is disruptive in class. She taps her ruler on the desk, and the noise is distracting. She also had two or three explosive outbursts when the kids were supposed to line up to go to the playground and also when they were told to put away their workbooks. The teacher thinks Samantha might have ADHD or maybe something worse, like bipolar illness." Ray looked worried as he told me this.

"Does Samantha have problems at home or just at school?" I asked. Just then Ray's cell phone rang. He looked at the screen. "Sorry," he said apologetically, "I forgot to turn it off. It will just take a second." He fiddled with the phone and finally turned off the ringer. He put the phone back in his briefcase.

"Uh, where were we? Oh, yes, Samantha has problems at home too. She gets very irritable when my wife tries to help her with her homework. She'll throw the homework on the floor and scream at her, 'You don't know anything.' Then she'll start crying and run to her room. We worry about her abrupt mood swings. She'll suddenly get angry for no reason that we can see." Ray sighed and continued.

"This has been very hard on my wife. She has chronic fatigue syndrome and chronic back pain. It's very difficult for her to deal with Samantha."

"Does Samantha do better with you helping her with homework?"

"Maybe a little. The problem is that I don't get home from work until after seven o'clock. I don't have that much time to help her because I usually have to cook dinner."

"Perhaps a tutor would help. Sometimes that takes away the power struggle with parents over homework." Ray thought a tutor was a good idea. He said he would talk this over with his wife.

"Uh," he hesitated. "I don't know if it's relevant, but maybe you should also know that we're in marriage counseling. We haven't been happy for a long time. Heidi has such a gloomy outlook on life. She constantly complains about her health. A few years ago, she went to a therapist and he wanted her to take antidepressants. But she's very antimedication, and she wouldn't go that route. Nothing I do or say seems to make her happy. Sometimes I feel totally controlled by her health problems and her negativity. Honestly, if it weren't for Samantha, I think we would have separated." Ray seemed sad as he told me this. Then he added, "I suppose I should also tell you that we've taken Samantha to two other child therapists. She improved for a short time, but now her behavior is worse than ever."

This statement raised a red flag for me. Did the other therapists fail because they focused only on Samantha and didn't address the problem in the family? Or were Samantha's parents resistant to taking good advice? I thought I'd better address this fairly soon.

"Well, I'll try to help. Of course, I'm not sure I'll succeed in helping your daughter if two other therapists have failed." In predicting I might not be able to help, I was putting myself one-down with Ray. As we'll see, this stance of humility sometimes helps in countering resistance.

Then I asked Ray if his wife complained about her health in front of Samantha.

"All the time," Ray said. Here's another red flag, I thought. We've seen with Alex and with Elizabeth how a parent's health problems can affect a child. Alex was the little boy who was worried that his father didn't have an "occupation" after he broke his arm; Elizabeth was the girl who was overly concerned about her mother's health.

Ray continued. "Samantha is very sympathetic to her mother. She's always asking if she can bring her a cool cloth for her forehead or a glass of water." His voice trailed off. Did Ray approve of Samantha's hearing her mother complain so much? I wondered. I suggested we schedule a meeting with the whole family.

The following week I greeted Ray, Heidi, and Samantha in the waiting room. Heidi was stunning, with perfectly bobbed blond hair and hazel eyes. Samantha was a younger, livelier version of her mother. For all her attractive appearance, though, Heidi had an air of unhappiness about her. Her face was pale and she seemed nervous about meeting me.

"So what's the trouble?" I asked when they had settled into my office.

"My teacher is mad at me," Samantha offered.

"Why is that?" I asked.

"I make noise in class." She looked at her mother. Heidi nodded.

"Do you like school?" I asked Samantha.

"Not lately."

"It's hard even getting her in the car to go to school," Heidi interjected.

"Heidi, just let Samantha answer," Ray said, a trace of impatience in his voice.

"I like seeing my friends at school," Samantha said finally.

I decided that it was time for me to talk with Samantha privately. I asked her parents' permission, and they agreed.

When Samantha and I were settled in the office and playing a game of Uno, I asked her my usual question to children: was she more worried about her mother or about her father.

"I'm mad, not worried." Samantha said, slapping down a card. Well, this was an interesting response, I said to myself. Not many children answer like this. Some kids hesitate and ask, "What do you mean?" Others say, "My parents are worried about *me*." Only a very few respond like Samantha—that they are mad, not worried.

Then Samantha added, more predictably, "Well, I'm more worried about my mommy because her back always hurts. She just lies in bed most of the day. I feel sad for her. And she argues with my daddy a lot. He has to cook dinner most nights because she can't stand up that long."

"I understand why you're worried," I said. After a pause, I asked, "And what makes you mad?"

"I *hate* when Mommy helps me with my homework. She goes too fast. And she doesn't even understand my homework." Samantha was discarding her cards quickly. She's an expert at this game, I thought.

"Would you like Daddy to help you with your homework instead of Mommy?"

"No. I don't want anyone to help me. Well," she was thinking this over, "maybe Daddy could help me a little. He knows more than Mommy."

We finished our game. I asked Ray and Heidi to join us for a few minutes. I wanted Samantha to see that I was a kind person who was going to help her parents so that she didn't have to. Samantha played quietly on the floor with a dollhouse while I spoke with Ray and Heidi. I first suggested that Ray help Samantha with her homework until they found a tutor, if they both agreed that a tutor was the way to proceed. Heidi said that Ray had brought up the idea of a tutor and she agreed that it would be a good thing. Ray said he would try to come home a little earlier so he'd have time to work with Samantha. I asked the parents to come back alone for the next session. Then, before the session was over, I gave Ray and Heidi a few written recommendations that I thought would be helpful. I said that we could go over them at the next session, which would be with them alone.

At the beginning of the next session, I asked Ray and Heidi if they were in agreement about the rules for Samantha. How did they deal with Samantha's outbursts at home? What did they do when she wouldn't get in the car to go to school? Did they give her consequences or punishments for misbehavior? Heidi and Ray said that they threatened to take away television time and video game time, and sometimes those worked to get her into the car in the morning. But enforcing the rules was such a battle that they didn't always follow through. For example, Heidi was tired and needed a break in the late afternoons, so she often allowed Samantha to watch television even if she had threatened to take it away.

I suggested that they make a firm rule about this and follow through. Samantha had to be in the car by 8:15 or else she would lose TV time and video game time that day. No exceptions. The same would hold true for temper tantrums. If Heidi needed a break, she could hire a teenager to babysit for Samantha in the late afternoons. They thought this might work, and Ray offered to ask at their church for a teenager who wanted to babysit.

So far, so good, I thought. But a tough item was coming up next on my list.

"I'd like to suggest that neither one of you say anything negative about your health in Samantha's presence." At this, Heidi bristled visibly.

"I don't think children should be sheltered from reality," she said coldly.

Parents rarely objected so forcefully to my directives. Fortunately, I had dealt with this particular objection before.

"I respect your opinion," I told Heidi as soothingly as I could. "But I think that when a child is *having problems*, it's best for parents to shelter them. I know from experience with many children that worries about a parent's health can affect a child's behavior in unpredictable ways. Of course when a child is not having problems, parents should do what they think best for their child about this issue."

Heidi didn't say anything. I hoped I had gotten through to her.

I wasn't sharing all my thoughts on this subject with Heidi because I didn't want her to feel blamed for complaining about her aches and pains to her daughter. But the fact is, I think that the less a child hears about her parents' problems, the better. A parent's worries can become exaggerated in a child's mind. A mother's casual comment that she's nervous about the dental implant she's going to have the next day may linger in the child's memory long after the

Novocain has worn off. The mother may not even think to reassure the child that everything went well. And the child might be afraid to ask, thereby letting the worry fester in her mind. I believe children must be protected. But I did not want to say this to Heidi. I thought it was best for her to feel that I was, at least in part, agreeing with her point of view.

I continued. "I'd like to ask both of you to say positive things about your lives in Samantha's presence, such as, 'I feel really happy today' or 'I had a good workout at the gym today.' In fact it would be best to say to Samantha, at least once a day, 'I had a good day today because . . .' You fill in the blanks. Also, Samantha shouldn't hear anything negative about the other parent." I paused so they could think this over.

"On the positive side, I'd like you to make a list of Samantha's best qualities and tell her two or three good things about herself every day. Let's talk about them right here. What are the best things about your daughter?"

"She's very kind and very empathic," Ray offered.

"She's very bright," Heidi said. Together we made a list of Samantha's good qualities. In addition to being kind and empathic, Samantha was artistic, helpful, intelligent, and pretty. I thought focusing on the positive would be especially important for Samantha because there was so much negativity in her family.

With children and especially with teenagers who are having serious problems, the family often gets caught in a downward spiral of negativity and misery. Family life becomes what narrative therapists call "problem saturated." Having parents make positive comments to the child and creating simple "certificates of praise," lauding the child's good qualities, become especially important. Posting a certificate of praise on the refrigerator can work wonders in creating a new, more positive family story. A family doesn't have to be in therapy to use certificates to good advantage. They are an excellent tool for parents to use themselves with their young children and even teenagers.

Praise for a child should be targeted and realistic or the child won't believe she deserves the compliments. I recommend that parents give their child a certificate of praise for being helpful around the house in small ways—like feeding the cat or putting away toys without being asked. This does not mean that parents should say "good job" to a child who remembers to wash her hands before dinner. It means catching a child being especially good instead of giving the child attention only when she does something wrong.

Parents often need to use a powerful magnifying glass to discover their child's best qualities. They also need to focus on qualities apart from intelligence or academic excellence. Sometimes we forget that a child's good grades or sports awards are not the only achievements that make us proud. We can too easily overlook other praiseworthy qualities such as creativity or generosity or even promptness. A single mother whose fourteen-year-old daughter was getting D's and F's at school gave her daughter certificates of praise for preparing simple dinners that they both ate when she came home from work. This simple strategy went a long way in turning around the atmosphere of negativity that had sprung up between them. The girl had felt that her mother noticed her only when she was doing something wrong.

After Heidi, Ray, and I talked about certificates of praise, which they agreed was a terrific idea, I suggested using a star chart to reward Samantha's good behavior, as I had done with Alex and Joey.

"Should she be watching so much television?" Ray asked after we had discussed the star charts.

"She doesn't watch that much," Heidi objected. I knew she was thinking of the long afternoons when she needed a break from Samantha.

"Does she watch only children's shows on public television?" I asked. This is what I usually recommend to parents.

"Yes, mostly children's shows. But I like to watch the news after dinner," Ray said. "Sometimes Samantha sits next to me while she does her homework."

"The television could be distracting to her. Could you possibly download the evening news on your iPod and listen to it later?" I asked.

"I could do that," he said. I explained that with children who have attention and focusing problems, it's often best to limit distractions. By cutting down on electronic noise, parents can create the kind of home environment that is calming to an inattentive child.

"It'll help Samantha stay focused if you turn off the television while she's doing her homework," I said. "And maybe turn off cell phones during dinner and homework time." Hearing this, Heidi rolled her eyes.

"Ray lives on his cell phone," she said. I had seen that myself. Most parents turn off their phones when they come into my office, but Ray had left his on. I wondered how easy he'd find it to keep his phone off at homework time. Ray looked annoyed but said nothing. Our time was up. We made another appointment for them in three weeks.

"By then, you should see some improvement," I assured them. As it turned out, I was being naïve.

Three weeks later, Ray and Heidi came to the appointment. Ray reported matter-of-factly that although they were following all my recommendations, there had been no improvement whatsoever in Samantha's behavior. I expressed surprise, but Ray assured me that they were following my directions.

I was fairly certain that one or both of the parents were not implementing the strategies; if they were, there would be at least some change—if not huge improvement—after three weeks. I suspected that there was sabotage going on, either consciously or unconsciously.

A direct approach was not going to work with this family. So I decided that I would try a traditional paradoxical technique called the "incompetent therapist." I told Ray and Heidi that I didn't think I could help Samantha after all, and I apologized for failing. I confessed that Samantha's problems were so difficult that they had defeated me, as they had defeated her previous therapists. I recommended that they consult another therapist or possibly think about taking Samantha to a child psychiatrist to see if medication might help her. In fact, I told them, since they had already seen other therapists, medication might be the only solution.

At this, Heidi cringed. My suggestion of medication was making her uncomfortable, as I thought it would. Ray had let me know in the first session that they were opposed to medicating Samantha.

I was intentionally putting the parents in an awkward situation, sometimes called a "therapeutic double bind." They could find yet another therapist and move along the road to medication for Samantha, or they could follow my recommendations and prove me wrong in my declaration that I could not help their daughter. Either way, as Jay Haley used to say, they would prove me wrong and put me down. Jay compared the therapist taking a one-down position to a dog lying on its back and showing vulnerability to end a fight that it couldn't win.

Ray and Heidi thought about my comments and then said that they wanted one more session with me. I repeated that I didn't think I could help them; their daughter's difficulties had defeated me even though I had tried my best. But they insisted. And so, appearing very reluctant, I scheduled an appointment for them in two weeks, after I returned from vacation. But I reminded them that I was pessimistic, saying that if my recommendations hadn't worked by now, they probably wouldn't work at all. Of course, I was hoping they would rebel against this.

Two weeks later, Ray came to the session alone. He reported that there was "huge improvement with Samantha." Her mood swings were gone and she was behaving well at school and doing better on tests. They had found a math tutor, and she had gotten B's on the last two tests. The star chart was working too. Ray had taken Samantha to the frozen yogurt shop for a treat two weekends in a row. Surprisingly, Heidi was making great efforts not to complain about her back pain or fatigue in front of her daughter. Samantha seemed to be less concerned with her mother's health. She expressed interest in having more playdates.

Ray thought that my recommendations were helping after all, but Heidi didn't want to come to therapy anymore since Samantha was doing so well. They were going to continue marriage counseling. The counselor had encouraged Ray to pursue activities that would make him happier. He was now playing basketball on Sunday mornings, something he really enjoyed, and he had started going to the YMCA to swim two nights a week after dinner. He was creating a space between himself and Heidi that made him less vulnerable to her complaining and negativity. But he was still reaching out to her in positive ways by suggesting that they get a babysitter and go out to dinner and by thinking of interesting family excursions.

I reacted to Ray's report of Samantha's improvement with open-mouthed surprise. I was puzzled, I said, because I really hadn't expected to be able to help. But I was pleased to hear that I had helped Samantha even a little. I added that Ray and Heidi must be doing an especially good job of parenting, and that was probably what was helping Samantha most of all. Here I was deliberately empowering the parents so they would feel confident about dealing with Samantha's behavior in the future. And once again I was taking a one-down position.

At this point, I predicted that the change in Samantha's behavior might be only temporary. "Relapses are very typical when a child shows this much improvement so quickly," I warned, "even when parents are as conscientious as you and Heidi are." Ray listened closely.

By predicting a relapse, I was hoping the parents would again rebel against me and prove me wrong. Predicting or even encouraging a relapse is a typical family therapy maneuver. It tends to block a relapse from occurring because it poses a challenge to the parents and again mobilizes their resistance.

Milton Erickson had an ingenious way of encouraging a relapse. He would tell the parents to think back to the time when the child's problem was making them miserable, and see if there was anything from that experience that they wished to salvage. He was, of course, giving the child's symptom a positive meaning in the life of the family. He was also playing on a common theme in family therapy: focusing on their child's problem makes parents feel closer because they have to put aside their marital problems and work together to help the child they both love.

Ray said they would call me if Samantha had a relapse, but since there was so much improvement he didn't think they would have to. After two months, I checked in with Ray. Samantha was getting A's and B's and she was not acting out in class anymore. He also told me that marriage counseling was helping them a little. He and Heidi were talking more, and he had been able to get her to go on a weekend family trip to SeaWorld, which they all had enjoyed.

Another name for the incompetent therapist strategy is "the positive connotation of the symptom." This means that the therapist is joining the family at the level of the family system by acknowledging the power of the child's symptom in keeping the family stable. The symptom is viewed as positive because it is the glue that holds the family system together. Without a "problem child" to take care of, the marriage might fail.

Some people criticize strategic family therapists for using paradoxical techniques like the one I used with Samantha's parents. Critics say that these interventions are manipulative since the therapist is not being absolutely up front with the family. My response is that when parents consult me to help a child who is suffering, I feel responsible to try everything in my capacity to help—without doing harm. Every therapist knows that many people resist the therapist's recommendations and sabotage the therapy. When that happens in family therapy, a therapist must focus on the well-being of the child and, if necessary, use indirect interventions with the parents to bring about therapeutic change.

I believe that parents who come to therapy truly have their children's best interests at heart, and some part of them wants therapy to work. Otherwise they wouldn't spend their time and money on therapy. When I use the incompetent therapist strategy, I feel that I am joining the healthy part of the parent, the part that really wants to bring about change, so that together we can overcome the part of their personality that is rebellious and resistant to authority. In fact, of course, the strategy of the incompetent therapist always contains a kernel of truth. I genuinely do feel I've failed if several sessions of family therapy have not produced positive results for a child.

The grand master of paradoxical techniques like the one I used with Samantha's family was Milton Erickson. Erickson had a personal understanding of a patient's need to rebel. When he was stricken with polio as a child, his doctors predicted he would never walk again. Erickson stubbornly defied their prognosis. After his first year at college, Erickson spent his summer vacation taking a thousand-mile river trip. When he started the trip, he did not have enough strength in his legs to pull his canoe out of the water, and he could swim only a few feet. On the river, he had to fish and forage for his own food since he had few supplies and only $2.32 in cash. With his considerable interpersonal skills, Erickson had no trouble getting fishermen and other travelers to give him the food he could not get on his own. By the end of the summer, he could swim a mile and carry his own canoe. Later in his life, Erickson needed a wheelchair to get around. But that was only after many years of proving his doctors wrong.

Erickson designed many strategies that make good use of patients' rebelliousness against their doctors. He often told his patients to have more of the very symptom they were trying to overcome. He was counting on their rebelling against his instructions and in fact having less of the symptom. Erickson worked with adults and children, and he devised creative, paradoxical strategies for both groups.

A good example of Erickson's prescribing the problem behavior was his intervention with a sixteen-year-old girl who sucked her thumb, much to the embarrassment of her parents and the irritation of her teachers. The school counselor had told Erickson that she thought the girl's thumb sucking was an aggressive act, intended to annoy her parents and other adults. So Erickson suggested that the girl become even more aggressive and really get in her parents' face. He instructed that every night the girl suck her thumb noisily for an hour in front of her mother and for another hour in front of her father. He also suggested that she suck her thumb in the class in which she most disliked the teacher. Erickson knew that being told to suck her thumb even more aggressively would take away its appeal.

At the same time, Erickson made the girl's parents promise not to react or try to limit her thumb sucking in any way while she was in treatment. The absence of a negative reaction on her parents' part also removed the girl's interest in the problem behavior since she was deliberately trying to annoy her parents and embarrass them by sucking her thumb at church and in other public places. After four weeks, the girl stopped sucking her thumb entirely and became interested in activities more typical for a teenager.

With the thumb-sucking girl, Erickson prescribed the problem behavior to the patient herself to sidestep her resistance. Another common technique for therapists who work with children is to have parents prescribe the problem behavior to their child or teenager, hoping the child will rebel against the parent. I used this technique with Joey when I asked his mother to supervise him in "not going to bed," and with Elizabeth when I asked her mother to ask Elizabeth to wash her hands even more. In both cases, as with Erickson's thumb-sucking teenager, holding on to the problem behavior became much more of an ordeal for the child than giving it up.

Utilizing the rebelliousness of his patients by prescribing the symptom is a very different approach to human problems than the one Erickson learned in medical school. In the 1930s, psychiatry in the United States was dominated by Freudian psychodynamic theory, and Erickson would have been well trained in this method. But being the rebellious person he was, Erickson adopted a different stance toward his patients. He made no attempt to uncover the "hidden meaning" behind the girl's odd behavior; nor did he explore with the girl why she was sucking her thumb at the unseemly age of sixteen. He did not attempt to help her understand why she maintained a behavior that she knew was terribly embarrassing to her parents. Early family therapists like Erickson realized that helping patients achieve insight about their problem did not produce change, especially in a rebellious or resistant teenager.

As for the "reason" for the thumb sucking, a traditional psychodynamic therapist might have posited that the girl was seeking to soothe herself because she was not receiving the nurturing she needed from her parents. Or he might have interpreted the behavior as an angry attempt to get back at her parents for their lack of nurturing. Therapy would focus on increasing the girl's awareness of how her thumb sucking was related to her childhood experiences and fantasies.

But Erickson was less interested in the psychological underpinnings of a symptom than he was in finding ways to get rid of it. He writes compellingly about another patient of his, a seventh-grade boy who couldn't read. His parents had tried everything to help him. They bought books for him and offered encouragement. They deprived him of all the things he enjoyed to try to force him to read. They had him tutored privately all through the summer, but when school started in fall the boy still couldn't read.

In the first therapy session, Erickson told the boy that he wasn't going to teach him how to read, as his parents had requested. Instead, he engaged the boy in a discussion of what he enjoyed doing most. This turned out to be fishing with his father. Where did the father fish? asked Erickson. Colorado, Washington, and California, answered the boy. Erickson then got out maps and together they located the towns in which the boy's father had fished. We are not reading the map, Erickson assured the boy; we are just looking for the names of towns. Erickson thus ingeniously reframed "reading" as "looking." When Erickson started to "make mistakes"—searching for a Colorado town in California or a Washington town in Colorado—the boy quickly jumped in to point out the right location of the town. But he was still not reading; he was correcting his therapist.

At this point Erickson engaged the boy in a conversation about fishing, and they pored over the map to find all the good fishing spots. Erickson even got out an encyclopedia so they could look up different kinds of fish.

Erickson worked with this boy all the following summer. When the boy announced that a reading test to determine his grade level was looming at the end of August, Erickson suggested they play a joke on his parents and teachers. The boy was to carefully make mistakes in reading the first-grade book, but to do better on the second-grade reader and even better on the third. Then Erickson instructed him to do an exceptional job on the eighth-grade reader. The boy thought this was a wonderful joke and did as Erickson directed. Later, he played truant and went to visit Erickson to tell him how amazed his parents and his teacher had been. He thought their trick was great fun.

Two paradoxical techniques play a part in this story, both of them directed at the child, not the parents. First, Erickson got the boy to read the map by not reading it. Then, by directing the boy to make intentional mistakes on his test, he was prescribing the symptom.

Together these indirect strategies bypassed the boy's resistance and helped him feel like a winner because he was able to put one over on his parents and his teacher.

When I was in graduate school, I lived in a dangerous neighborhood on the south side of Chicago. Since I was not very strong physically, I decided to learn a martial art so that I would have some means of protection in case I found myself in a threatening situation. I joined the university judo club and practiced judo for three years. The idea behind judo is to use your opponent's own strength and momentum to defeat him. I have often been struck by the idea that using the strength of a client's resistance to defeat his problem relies on this same principle.

Helping young people with "resistant" parents who sabotage the therapy was something that Freud found daunting a hundred years ago. He describes a fascinating case of a young agoraphobic girl who was afraid to leave her house and was also afraid to stay at home alone. The girl's parents brought her to Freud for psychoanalysis. In the process of treatment, the girl confided to Freud that her mother was having an improper relationship with a well-to-do gentleman who was a friend of their family. When the girl made the mistake of mentioning to her mother that she knew about the affair and had discussed it with Freud, her mother pulled her out of treatment and sent her to an institution, where the unfortunate girl remained for many years. Freud declared this girl a notable failure of psychoanalysis.

Although Freud did not realize it, his patient's agoraphobia had a protective function in her family. The girl was protecting her father by having the symptom. As long as her mother had to stay at home with her daughter, she would have fewer opportunities to go out to meet her lover. Her mother, of course, did not want her affair to become known, so she sabotaged the therapy.

The meaning that Freud took from this case was that the intervention of parents was a danger to psychoanalytic treatment, and one he did not know how to address. Freud knew how to deal with inner resistance—by helping the patient gain insight—but he lamented that he did not know how to deal with what he called "resistance from outside." This was a cornerstone of a strong tradition in psychoanalytic therapy: excluding the patient's family members from therapy in order to prevent their sabotaging the treatment. It was not until the 1950s that therapists started to view problems like agoraphobia from an interpersonal perspective, and were led to invent paradoxical strategies to deal with resistant parents. Freud was of course working from an individual perspective. A family therapist would have involved the parents of Freud's agoraphobic young woman from the very beginning.

Erickson used paradoxical techniques with children, but he was also keenly aware of how their family relationships played a part in their symptoms. With the thumb-sucking girl and the boy who couldn't read, it was only by mobilizing their rebellion against their parents that Erickson was able to bring about change.

Erickson doesn't tell us how these young people fared once their symptoms were gone, or how these changes affected other family members. But we do know that Erickson and the other early family therapists made a prophetic observation: If the underlying family issues are not addressed, another family member may develop symptoms, sometimes months or even years later.

In the next chapter, we see what happens when parents end a child's therapy before resolving the deeper family issues.

SEVEN

Medication

The Promise and the Peril

UNHAPPINESS IN A FAMILY can make itself known in all sorts of ways. A first-grade boy becomes hyperactive; a ten-year-old girl is suddenly paralyzed by worry and anxiety; a teenager withdraws to her room in sullen despair. In the family therapist's worldview, these symptoms are outcroppings of a deep river of discontent flowing in the family. The child with symptoms is merely the "identified patient," the one who carries the pain for the whole family. From this perspective, therapy must shift focus, as we have seen, from the child's problems to the parents' difficulties—whether it's day-to-day bickering, frosty distance, or outright anger and contempt.

What happens, then, if the child's symptoms are treated with medication—say, Ritalin or Adderall for the hyperactivity or Zoloft for the depression? The hyperactive boy may indeed calm down and the depressed girl may well cheer up. But, as we will see, if the deeper

family issues are not addressed and resolved, unanticipated consequences may emerge, sometimes months or even years later.

The unhappiness in six-year-old Matt's family took the form of
violence. Matt hit and bit other children at kindergarten, and one day
he threw a book at his teacher, narrowly missing her eye. She quickly
dispatched a classroom aide to walk Matt to the principal's office,
but they were barely out the door when Matt ran off. Somehow he
found a way through the fence that surrounded the school. He was
about to dash into the street when a teacher supervising recess in the
playground managed to catch him and escorted him to the principal's
office.

The principal promptly called Matt's mother at work. While they
waited for her to come and take Matt home, the assistant principal
and the physical education teacher had to hold Matt down so he
wouldn't run away again. When his mother arrived, Matt was sob-
bing and screaming for them to let him go. That day, Matt's mother,
Francine, called me to make an appointment.

I saw Matt and his parents the next morning. When I greeted the
family in the waiting room, Matt was playing a video game on his
Game Boy. Francine, looking tense and drawn, was reading a paper-
back novel, and her husband, Sam, was e-mailing on his BlackBerry.
I introduced myself and invited them into my office. Matt sat on the
couch next to his mother and continued to play his game, hardly
looking up. Sam sat across from them on the love seat.

Francine was small and thin, with short red hair and pale skin.
She worked part-time in a doctor's office. The rest of the time she
was a "soccer mom," driving Matt and his ten-year-old sister, Paige,
to their after-school activities. Sam, an attorney, was tall with dark
brown hair and dark-rimmed glasses. Matt, with his dark hair and
dark eyes, resembled his father. Sam launched into an explanation of
what happened at school.

"Matt told us that another boy hit him, and that's why he got angry and hit back. He ran away because he thought he was going to get into trouble for hitting."

"Is that what happened?" I asked Matt.

"Alan hit me first," Matt said, finally looking up from his game.

"But this isn't the first time it's happened," Sam said. "Any little thing seems to make him angry. And then he overreacts. We're worried that he might be bipolar or have ADHD. One minute he's fine, and the next minute he gets really angry. I used to train dogs, and we had an expression called the "red zone" for when a dog was out of control. Well, Matt goes into the 'red zone' and we can't pull him out of it."

While Sam was talking, I was starting to wonder about the deeper currents of hostility in this family, since a child's aggressive acting out is more often than not a metaphor for hostility between his parents.

"We had a meeting at the school a month ago with Matt's teacher, the principal, and the school psychologist," said Francine. "The teacher told us he's distracted in the classroom. He can't focus on his assignments; he wanders over to other children's desks. And sometimes he pokes or pushes them. And now with this incident . . ." She paused and ran her fingers through her hair in a gesture of frustration. "I mean, throwing a book at a teacher is really out of bounds. And running away—where did he think he would go? What was he thinking? We're very worried," she added. Then she said, "The school psychologist thought he might need medication."

Sam and Francine seemed to be amiable people and were obviously very worried about their son. Sam worked in the city, and he was taking half a day off to come to therapy. I wondered where Matt's extreme behavior was coming from. He was certainly riveting his parents' attention onto him, deflecting their thoughts from some other troubling issue. This might well be his parents' unhappiness in their marriage or it might be something else.

"We don't really want to go the medication route if we can avoid it.

We've read that ADHD drugs can have terrible side effects on kids," Sam continued. "The teacher has him on a plan with rewards for good behavior. But she thinks that might not be enough for him."

By this point, I noticed that Matt had gotten restless and wandered over to inspect the toy shelves. Then he crossed the room to sit next to his father and started fiddling with his BlackBerry.

"Is Matt angry at home as well as school?" I asked.

"Sometimes he gets angry at Paige and hits her," Francine said, "so we try to separate the two of them as much as possible. And Matt takes forever to do his homework. He sometimes gets frustrated and then angry and throws papers on the floor. Can you imagine? He actually has homework in kindergarten." Matt attended a private school where they believed in "challenging" the children.

"Paige always starts the fights. She picks on me and breaks my toys," Matt interjected.

Sibling squabbles are common in families. But if these conflicts are severe and chronic, I suspect they reflect a battle that is raging between the parents. I would have to see Francine and Sam alone. But for now I decided to give them some parenting strategies.

I suggested that they not yell at Matt but calmly state the consequences for misbehavior and then calmly enforce them. They said taking away his Game Boy and Nintendo seemed to work if they stood their ground. But losing his video games often sent Matt into a meltdown. He would cry and scream for an hour until Francine couldn't take it anymore and gave in.

Matt has learned that tantrums are a source of power in his family, I said to myself. He wasn't going to give them up so easily. I would need to try a paradoxical strategy to avoid a power struggle that would only send Matt into a meltdown.

I turned to Sam and Francine and said matter-of-factly, "Matt needs to 'practice' having tantrums." I went on to explain. Twice a day, for fifteen minutes, Matt would have to stay in his room and pound a pillow and scream, just as though he were having a tantrum. Francine would supervise this during the day, and in the evenings Sam would take over. Matt's tantrums would thus come under the control of his parents, who told him when, where, and how long to have them.

At first, Sam and Francine seemed taken aback by the idea of a pretend tantrum, but they quickly got into the spirit of it and agreed to follow my directions.

"We're going to try this right here," I announced. I took a lion-shaped pillow from the couch and gave it to Matt.

"You mean right now?" Matt asked.

"Yes, right now. Francine, please tell Matt to punch the pillow hard. And tell him to make a lot of noise while he's doing it, just like he does at home when he has a tantrum." Matt held on to the pillow and stared at me in silence.

"Matt, punch that pillow. Pretend that I took away your Game Boy and you're mad," Francine told him. Matt sat still and said nothing.

"Sam, could you go over and sit next to Francine?" I said. Sam got up and went over to sit next to his wife. Then I told Matt to take his father's place. He stood up, pillow in hand, and moved to the love seat.

"Now, Sam, back up Francine. Tell Matt to pretend to be angry and punch that pillow." I wanted Matt to see that his parents formed a united front to take charge of his behavior. That's why I got them to sit together on the couch. Having people change seats in a session is a typical family therapy tactic. The new seating arrangement symbolically represents the new hierarchy that the therapist is working to establish in the family. My goal here was to create a spatial boundary around the parents, indicating that they were the executive leaders of the family organization, with Matt in the position of a subordinate who had to obey his parents' directions. The family therapist may sometimes direct a parent who is underinvolved with a child to sit closer to the child, or move an overinvolved parent to the other side of the room, as far as possible from the child. The therapist is like a stage director, utilizing spatial position to amplify meaning.

Sam, now sitting next to his wife, backed up her instructions. "Go ahead, Matt," he said. Matt resisted for a few minutes. Then he gave the pillow a light punch. The three of us encouraged him to punch harder and get really angry. He punched a little harder.

"I'm tired of this," Matt said finally, throwing down the pillow.

As I had hoped, his parents directing him made Matt lose interest in having a tantrum. I was also happy to see that both parents were backing each other up. Sometimes one parent might object, claiming that he didn't see the point of the tactic. But Sam and Francine were able to work together toward a common goal—at least in my office.

Our time was drawing to a close, so I gave the parents a few of my usual recommendations. I also passed on a tip that I had learned from the mother of two feisty boys. I told Francine that the next time Matt and Paige were fighting and claiming that the other one had started it, she was to say, "No, *I* started it." This is so surprising to kids that it can stop them in their tracks. Surprise and novelty are important tools for parents because they change the game just enough for the child to wonder what is going on.

Children, like teenagers, like to push parents' buttons and wait for the predictable response. So rather than just trying more of what doesn't work—like yelling at kids or threatening them with punishment—I often recommend that parents try something novel and unpredictable to get their kids to stop fighting. One tactic is for parents to purchase three plant sprayers. The next time the children start fighting, the parent challenges them to a "water duel." This cuts the tension and brings humor into a strained situation. A variation is for parents to keep a Halloween wig or a mask handy and challenge the child to a water duel after putting on the mask.

I suggested that Francine supervise Matt in a "helping chore" appropriate for a six-year-old, such as wiping off the refrigerator or picking up toys from the family room. Helping chores are especially useful when a child is protecting a parent by having a symptom. Doing a chore gives the child a more productive way of helping. I also suggested that the parents ask the teacher to create a "calm down" corner in the classroom or even in the principal's office for Matt to sit in when he got into an argument with a classmate or became upset or angry. Fortunately, Matt's school was more than happy to cooperate.

Finally, I urged Matt's parents to limit media stimulation at home. Singing cell phones and buzzing BlackBerries, loud television shows and blaring commercials, Game Boys and computer games all compete for our children's attention—and our own. Sometimes parents don't realize how distracting electronic noise can be to a child who is trying to read or do his homework or even think about what he wants to do next. If parents are concerned that their child might have ADHD, I recommend that they limit TV watching to a maximum of one hour per day of public television only. Public television provides quality programming for kids, usually with educational content and without violence or inappropriate language.

The American Academy of Pediatrics (AAP) recommends that parents limit screen time, including TV, movies, video games, and computer games, to a total of "one to two hours a day" for children ages two and over. For children under the age of two, they recommend no screen time at all. They also suggest that the TV be turned on only for a particular program and turned off when it's over, and that parents set a good example by limiting their own TV viewing and by choosing programs carefully. Another AAP recommendation is that parents should not put a TV in their children's bedrooms or allow them to do their homework with the TV on.

The AAP points out that exposure to media violence can contribute to mental health problems in children and adolescents. They warn parents that children who watch violence on TV are more likely to engage in aggressive behavior. Psychologist Martha Stout, an expert on childhood trauma, tells us that media violence is nothing less than a traumatic assault on the consciousness of our children. She points out that unfortunately children routinely witness violence in some form. Even children from sheltering families who live far from inner cities are assailed by graphic television and movie images of car crashes, kidnappings, and war. I have seen children experience night terrors after watching a violent or scary television show before bed. Even classic children's movies like *Snow White* or *Bambi* may be terrifying to a four-year-old.

Passively witnessing violence on television is not as harmful as suffering physical or sexual abuse, but it can still be traumatic. Also, just hearing parents call each other names and hurl insults at each other can be more disturbing to a child than most parents realize. How disturbing this is depends on the individual child's experience and sensitivity, but most kids are acutely aware and even vigilant about their parents' fighting. That's why I am so adamant about parents' keeping their conflicts out of the hearing and sight of their children. I also make strong efforts to convince parents to keep violent video games, movies, and television shows out of their child's life. This usually calls for making some changes at home, and it also means that parents need to talk with the parents of their child's friends to agree on what programs are acceptable.

These seem like simple commonsense suggestions, hardly profound life changers. But in fact I have discovered that reducing media distractions—violent or not—can actually do wonders to help a child become calmer and focus better in school and at home. It also allows parents to tune in to their child and have uninterrupted conversations with him. The earlier parents start limiting electronic distractions, the easier it is to enforce those limits later on.

Apart from the violent content of many electronic games, having access to instant entertainment in all their leisure hours deprives children of the opportunity to use their own imagination. One of the things that I learned early on in working with children is that they love to create their own games and invent new rules for existing games. Children, left to their own devices, can entertain themselves for hours with a handful of toy cars or crayons and paper. Playing video games invented by adults offers little challenge to a child's imagination.

For all these reasons, some brave parents have elected not to have any television viewing in their homes. Some have a monitor screen on which they and their children can watch videos and movies, which the parents choose and limit. Other parents don't have screens of any kind. When my own children were young, our next-door neighbors chose not to have a television or videos in their home. They did allow their three children to watch an hour of public television at our house, and at 5:00 every evening there were six children huddled in front of our tiny TV screen watching *Sesame Street*. Once in a while, the neighbor children were allowed to watch a Disney movie at our house as well. These children were happy, well-adjusted kids, and I never heard them complain about not having television at home. And why would they, when their parents were always available for an after-dinner game of Crazy Eights or Connect Four or a bike ride in the park? Many parents I've talked to report that home life is much richer without the constant din of entertainment and commerce that characterizes what one observer called the "electronic hearth." For these families, a real hearth—not just a fireplace, but family games, music, conversation, even shared hobbies—occupies a central place in their family life.

At the opposite extreme, some parents are so accustomed to having multiple televisions in their homes and even in their children's bedrooms that they can't imagine how they would be able to remove them. My suggestions that they simply donate their televisions to a charity or disconnect the TV cable are met with looks of bewilderment and words of protest. These parents feel powerless in the face of our society's unconditional acceptance of technology. They feel that their child is entitled to a television in his room, as well as to the latest versions of PlayStations, Nintendos, and Xboxes. Some parents have asked me whether their thirteen- and fourteen-year-old sons should be allowed access to Internet porn sites. Aghast that they would even ask such a question, I try to spell out for them that porn is an addictive and dangerous pastime unsuited to teenagers, and can even be traumatizing.

Limiting or reducing "screen time" is not easy. Television and video games are so seductive—for both children and adults—that even the most imaginative child can succumb to the temptation. Parents need to work hard to impose limits and become inventive at finding other things for their kids to do. For younger children, I recommend that parents and children sit down together and compose a list of fun activities—playing a game, reading, doing a jigsaw puzzle, painting or drawing, baking cookies, playing outside. They then write each activity on a slip of paper and put the papers in a large jar or box, which is called the "I have nothing to do" jar. When a child feels bored, he takes a slip of paper out of the jar and does the activity written on it.

Francine and Sam were willing to try limiting screen time for Matt and were generally accepting of my suggestions as far as their son was concerned. But as I got to know them better, I realized that their marriage was foundering. Our therapy sessions revealed deep resentments and power struggles. Francine had grown up in a family with a lot of love but little money. Sam's parents had been well off, but they had been controlling and not at all affectionate with their children. I could see that these issues were playing out in their marriage. Francine complained that Sam was too controlling. He made all the major decisions in their life—buying a car, choosing where they went on vacations, even deciding which house they bought. He insisted on picking out the furniture because he worried that Francine would be too extravagant. Francine accused Sam of bullying her and ordering her around like a servant. He sometimes went into a rage if she left the water running too long in the shower or if dinner wasn't served on time. I had the clear impression of an atmosphere of high tension and conflict.

Sam, in turn, opened up about his own anger, which dated back to when Paige was born. He felt that Francine had turned away from him at that point, giving all her affection first to Paige and later to Matt. He said he felt like he was in a daily competition with his children for his wife's attention. Seeing Francine placate Matt, instead of disciplining him consistently, made Sam furious. He thought that Francine was too indulgent with both children but especially with Matt, who badly needed firm limits.

Francine told me she sometimes defended Matt against Sam's harsh discipline, whereupon Sam would accuse her of undermining him and then stalk off to his study, leaving her to deal with the children. Embittered and estranged, the couple had grown apart while Francine and Matt grew closer—not a healthy boundary arrangement at all. Both Sam and Francine admitted that they screamed and fought at home, and, yes, sometimes the children did overhear them. They knew this had to change.

I've talked before about paradoxical interventions with children, but this technique can work with adults as well. At the end of my first therapy session with Sam and Francine, I prescribed a simple paradoxical intervention for them. From 7 a.m. to 9 a.m. and from 7 p.m. to 9 p.m., Sam would make all the family decisions—including decisions about the children and all household matters. The rest of the time, Francine would be in charge. This intervention is paradoxical because I am asking Sam to continue to make decisions for the family, but at a particular time of day. If I asked him to stop making all family decisions, he might well rebel. This intervention was aimed at giving Francine a feeling of being in charge at least some of the time. To help Sam feel more loved, I asked Francine to plan a romantic evening, during which she was to make Sam her highest priority. It could be in a restaurant or at home after the children were in bed.

Over the next few months, I continued to meet with Sam and Francine. Matt's behavior slowly improved. He wasn't getting into trouble at school, but his teacher said he was still too distracted to stay on task. His parents were being careful not to argue in front of the children, and they were supervising the practice tantrums, although Francine admitted that it was tough to get Matt to follow through for fifteen minutes. Meanwhile, they were enforcing the rules and not giving in to Matt's tantrums. They had made a star chart, and Matt had managed to earn his reward for three out of six weeks. Both Francine and Sam said they were a little happier with their marriage.

But they were still concerned about Matt's inability to focus. The school year was coming to a close, and, unlike some of the children in his class, Matt had not learned to read. I reassured them that many children don't read in kindergarten but quickly catch up later. I urged them not to worry.

Sam and Francine decided to take a break from therapy for the summer. When Matt started first grade, the same old problem returned: he was too inattentive to focus on his schoolwork. Although Matt was bright, he was still struggling with reading. His teacher was convinced that his attention problems would go away with medication and he would learn to read once his ADHD was addressed. Sam's sister, a psychiatrist, agreed.

Worn down and feeling hopeless, Francine and Sam reluctantly decided to try medication for Matt. Their pediatrician, after talking with Francine about Matt's school problems, prescribed the popular ADHD drug Adderall. Francine and Sam were still concerned about the side effects of weight loss and insomnia, but they felt they had no choice. And the school had promised that with this diagnosis Matt would be entitled to extra attention from a teacher's aide, which might well help to keep him focused.

A month later, when I called Francine for an update, she said that the Adderall seemed to be helping. Matt was focusing much better in the classroom and had started to read. "It's like a miracle," she said. They had decided to stop therapy since Matt's behavior was so much better. Were she and Sam still fighting? I wondered. Was the atmosphere at home still toxic? Francine made no mention of her and Sam's marital difficulties. I knew that there were still some unresolved issues in their marriage, which might mean trouble for the family later on. But the parents had made their decision, and I didn't question it. I wished them well. Privately, I hoped they would continue to contain their quarrels and practice the other techniques I had given them.

In the last few years, many parents have come to my office firmly opposed to medication and determined to find an alternative in family therapy. These parents—even those who are taking drugs themselves—have read reports of the research that point to dangerous side effects. Adderall XR (extended release), for example, is no longer prescribed in Canada because studies have identified a risk of sudden death in children who take it.

The U.S. Food and Drug Administration (FDA) examined the same research as the Canadian health authorities, but concluded that the risk of sudden death was not convincing enough to warrant pulling the drug from the market. However, the FDA demanded that a stronger warning, known as a "black box," be placed on the label of Adderall XR, Adderall, and other ADHD drugs. Shire Pharmaceuticals, the manufacturer of Adderall, stated that it agreed with the FDA's desire for more safety studies on Adderall but disagreed with the FDA advisory panel's recommendation that the drug be labeled with a "black box." Adderall's label currently warns, "Misuse of amphetamine may cause sudden death and serious cardiovascular adverse events." Typical side effects of Adderall in children include loss of appetite, difficulty falling asleep, stomachache, headache, weight loss, and dry mouth.

On college campuses in the United States, Adderall and other ADHD prescription medications are quickly becoming drugs of choice as study aids, replacing coffee and Coke. More and more college students are abusing Adderall, claiming that the drug improves concentration and increases stamina during long hours of study. Many assume that because the drug is legal for prescription use, it must be safe. According to recent studies, this is not the case at all. Matt was one of those kids for whom Adderall worked well to help him focus without causing serious side effects. But his appetite was affected, and he did lose some weight.

Five years passed with no word from Sam or Francine. Then one morning I got a call from Francine. She sounded frantic. Their daughter Paige, now fifteen, was depressed and had threatened to kill herself. I consider a suicide threat a serious emergency, and I told Francine that I would switch around some appointments so I could see Paige and her parents that very afternoon. Then I asked about Matt. He was getting B's in school, Francine said, and wasn't having any significant behavior problems. He was still taking Adderall. He had lost some weight and had trouble getting to sleep, but they believed it was worth it to have him doing so well in school.

Sam and Francine came with Paige to the appointment. Paige was dressed like the Goth high school crowd—black jeans, black sweatshirt, and more than a hint of dark purple eye shadow. Each of her ears was pierced in three places, and she wore little gold studs. Her brown hair was stringy, as though she hadn't washed it in a week, and she had black circles under her eyes. She slumped into a chair in my office, glancing down at the cell phone in her hand. She appeared to be texting as we began to talk.

"When did you start to feel depressed?" I asked Paige, ignoring her flying fingers on the phone. "About a year ago," she said, not meeting my eyes.

"Paige, I'd appreciate your putting your phone away, just for the short time you're here," I said quietly. Taking a last look at the screen, Paige turned off her phone and put it in her pocket.

I continued. "Thanks. Did anything else happen in your family around the time when you first started feeling down?" I asked. Teen depression often accompanies transitions or losses in family life, such as divorce or the illness or death of a relative.

Paige shrugged. "I don't think so."

"It was just after my father died," Francine said. "Do you think that her grandpa's death could have anything to do with her depression?"

"It might," I said. Hearing her mother cry could well be worrisome or even mildly traumatic to Paige. And the loss of her grandfather might have been a blow.

Just then—as though to change the somber subject—Paige interrupted and asked if she could talk with me alone. This did not surprise me: Teenagers are not known for wanting to share secrets with their parents. Sam and Francine left the office.

Paige didn't seem to have anything specific in mind to talk about, and we sat in silence for a moment. I was about to ask my usual question—which parent she was more worried about—when she suddenly began to cry and said softly, "I'm really worried about my mom."

"Why?" I asked, marveling at how she anticipated my question.

"She was so sad about my grandpa dying. She cried every day for a while. And she lost her job two years ago. So now she's home all the time. She and my dad are always fighting. Our house is like a war movie. I honestly think they should get a divorce. She would be better off."

I thought about this. Clearly, Sam and Francine were not following my advice not to fight or argue in front of the kids. They had managed this when Matt was the problem, but once his behavior was under control they apparently fell back on their old ways of relating to each other. This time Paige might be taking the hit for their anger. I considered the possibility that Paige's depression was a metaphor for her mother's sadness as well as for the hopelessness of her parents' marriage.

I asked Paige about her suicide threat. She told me she hated her life and felt like she had nothing to live for. Her father was really strict and made her come home at 10:00 p.m. on weekend nights. On school nights she wasn't allowed to be out past 8:00 p.m. unless she was at a school event.

"They treat me like a child. None of my friends have to be home at ten o'clock on Friday nights," Paige complained.

"Do you feel like killing yourself now?" I asked. Paige thought about this for a few moments. Then she answered, "No, not right now." I breathed a sigh of relief.

A teenager's suicide threat can be rooted in true emotional pain or it can be manipulative. Threatening suicide gives a teen a lot of power and can even be leveraged to get more privileges. Sometimes the threat can be both manipulative and genuine. Paige's preoccupation with suicide appeared to be rooted in real emotional pain, with perhaps a touch of manipulation.

Whatever the motivation, teen suicide threats have to be taken very seriously. Suicide is the third-leading cause of death among adolescents in the United States. About 20 percent of teens suffer depression before they reach adulthood, and about 8 percent of teens suffer depression for a year at a time as compared with 5.3 percent of the general population.

I asked Paige if she had thought about ways to kill herself or if she had a plan. She told me that sometimes she contemplated overdosing with pills, but she had no idea of what kind of pills she would take or where she would get them. Profound sadness and suicidal thinking put a youngster at real risk for carrying through with suicide, whether or not they have formulated a plan. One sixteen-year-old boy I was treating for depression impulsively swallowed a bottle of pain medication that he spotted at his grandfather's house. He had never thought about this particular act before.

I asked Paige what usually helped her feel better when she was depressed. She told me that when she was out with friends or at a friend's house, she didn't feel so much pain. Sometimes just talking to a friend on the phone or even instant messaging with a friend helped relieve her sadness.

I was glad to hear that Paige called a friend to ask for help when she needed it. It's the teens who are isolated with few or no friends who are more seriously at risk. Today many teens, especially in homes with two working parents and hectic schedules, spend more time talking with their peers than with their families. Their friends become a kind of second family, a family that is available to them more often—via text messaging, tweeting, Facebooking, and instant messaging—than their time-squeezed parents.

At the end of my session with Paige and her family, I made one appointment for her to see me alone and another appointment with her parents.

A child's suicide threat catapults a family into a state of crisis that demands immediate vigilance on the part of the whole family. My first step was to set up a twenty-four-hour suicide detail in which a parent or a grandparent would watch over Paige and not leave her alone at home. Her mother would sleep in her room at night. At school, where she said she didn't feel as depressed as she did at home, Paige would be surrounded by her classmates and teachers. Sometimes parents even accompany their suicidal kid to school and shadow him throughout the day if they and the therapist believe that the risk of suicide is really serious.

The suicide watch takes a lot of devotion and attention on the part of the parents, but I've found it's the best way to keep a child safe while I help resolve the family problems. Since my hypothesis was that Paige's suicide threat was also an attempt to distract her mother from her own sadness and marital difficulties, I would have to help her mother overcome these challenges.

When, five years earlier, Matt's violent behavior and learning problems had been resolved by his taking Adderall, I had worried that the underlying issues in the family—and especially the parents' troubled relationship—might affect Paige one day. It is often sadly true that the identified patient changes although the root cause of the disturbance in the family remains the same. As Minuchin has observed, when family sorrow gets to the point of producing symptoms, we think we know where the problem is. Parents can point to their teenager and say "she's the one with the problem; she's the one who is depressed." But the therapist reflects silently, "Don't be so sure." Just as pain can be deferred from one part of the body to another, so a parent's anguish can come out in a child.

When I asked Sam and Francine if they had stopped arguing in front of the children, Sam exclaimed impatiently, "What's that got to do with Paige's suicide threat? We're talking about a sick kid here, not about Francine's and my marriage." He added that his sister, who was a psychiatrist, thought that Paige had a "chemical imbalance" and needed antidepressants. I explained to Sam that antidepressants often increase the risk of suicide in adolescents. In March 2004, the FDA mandated that certain antidepressant drugs, such as Prozac, Paxil, and Zoloft, be labeled with "black boxes," warning that these drugs led to an increase in suicidal thinking in patients. I told Sam that I preferred to treat Paige's depression with family therapy.

Sam finally agreed to come in for five sessions and then reevaluate. But I had the feeling he was trying to take charge of his daughter's therapy. If he did, therapy would surely fail. Undermining the therapist's authority is one way that a family resists the painful process of changing their relationships. A systems explanation for this resistance is that the family in pain must have a symptomatic child so that the deeper pain in the family—in this case the parents' marital unhappiness—doesn't get addressed. Early family therapists, borrowing a term from systems theory, called a family's resistance to change "homeostasis." In order to maintain homeostasis or equilibrium, the family has to have a symptomatic member who serves as a focal point for everyone's attention. Unfortunately, that role now fell to Paige.

Over the next month, I tried all sorts of strategies with this family. To create a more upbeat environment at home, I asked the parents to make a list of Paige's positive qualities and sprinkle them into their conversations with her. They also made a certificate of praise to celebrate Paige's good grades. This did help to drain away some of the negativity at home.

As they worked together to help Paige, Sam and Francine were talking to each other more and had gone out to lunch a couple of times while the children were in school. They had both enjoyed the romantic evening at an Italian restaurant that Francine had planned.

I was beginning to breathe easier about Paige's depression. Then one night I got an emergency call from Francine. Paige and her father had gotten into a terrible argument and Paige had tried to cut her wrists. I was stunned by this setback and wanted to meet with Paige and her parents as soon as possible. At this point, Sam was insistent that they take Paige to a child psychiatrist for medication, but he and Francine also hoped they could see me the next day if that was possible.

Paige and both parents came to the session. Paige had made scratches on her wrists with her mother's sewing scissors, but I could see that the cuts were superficial. To me, it looked more like a gesture, a cry for help, than an actual suicide attempt. Paige told me that she was furious at her father for insisting she come home at 11 p.m. from a friend's birthday party, which was the following Saturday. Her father wouldn't let her sleep over at the party even though two of her friends were sleeping over. She could see no good reason for his restrictions—she didn't drink or use drugs. Paige accused her father of treating her like a child and keeping her on a "leash." What she was telling me was not so different from her mother's complaints about Sam's controlling and bullying her, I thought.

As Paige spoke, Sam got so angry that he stormed out of my office. "This is so typical," Paige said. "If he doesn't get his way, he has a tantrum. I'm sick and tired of dealing with him." Francine was silent. She looked as though she were about to cry. The session was over anyway, and when Francine and Paige went downstairs, they found Sam waiting in the car.

Later that day, Sam took Paige to a psychiatrist, who talked with her privately for an hour. At the end of the session, the doctor came into the waiting room and told the frightened parents that she believed Paige was actively suicidal and should be hospitalized immediately. Both parents, shocked by the suicide attempt, agreed to hospitalization.

During her five days in the hospital, Paige was evaluated as seriously at risk for taking her own life. She was given antidepressants, and she attended individual and group therapy each day. On the last day, her parents joined her for a group family therapy session, at which they discussed some of the issues that Paige was so angry about. Her father agreed to extend her curfew on weekends if that would help her feel better. In return, she agreed to sign a contract for safety, saying that if she began to think about suicide, she would let one of her parents know at once. These contracts for safety, also called anti-suicide contracts, are typically used when a teenager is at risk for self-harm. In addition, Paige's therapist asked her parents to suicide-proof their house—locking away scissors, knives, and medications that could be potentially harmful.

After Paige was released from the hospital, Sam insisted that she continue to see the psychiatrist for medication and also a therapist whom his sister recommended for individual talk therapy. He didn't think family therapy was helping. I had to agree with him. I hadn't been able to make much headway with the parents' marriage. This family's stubborn resistance to change had unfortunately not yielded to my interventions.

Over the next few months, I kept in touch with Francine, and learned that two months after her first hospitalization, Paige had been hospitalized a second time for her own safety. The doctors had doubled her dosage of medication and added a second antidepressant. But Paige continued to feel depressed; as sometimes happens with antidepressants, the drugs were not working. She made two more suicide gestures, cutting her wrists first with a safety pin and then with a paper clip. Eventually, Sam and Francine had no further options but to place Paige in a residential treatment facility in a nearby state. She seemed to be doing well there when her parents visited her. A few months after Paige entered residential treatment, Francine and Sam separated.

The resentments between Sam and Francine had been festering for so long that family therapy was not able to save their marriage. They were caught up in a struggle that neither could win. If they had worked through their painful marriage problems when they first brought their son to me, instead of Band-Aiding Matt's problems with medication, perhaps there might have been more hope. I have helped other families tackle their problems early on so that their smoldering discord doesn't turn into a conflagration.

One such family came to see me after their fourteen-year-old son, Adam, was discharged from the hospital following a week's stay for depression and oppositional defiant disorder. His parents, Lisa and Bob Crystal, had been referred to me by their insurance company. Like many parents, they came in alone to meet me first, the day before Adam was to be released from the hospital. They were a pleasant couple in their forties who had been married for twenty years. Bob worked from home for a property management company and Lisa was a high school English teacher. They had three children: Jason, seventeen, Adam, fourteen, and Brenda, ten. Lisa and Bob both seemed at a loss as to how to help Adam.

Lisa explained to me that before he was hospitalized, Adam had been in individual therapy for eight months. His therapist became frightened when Adam repeatedly told her he "just wanted to die." The therapist referred Adam to a psychiatrist, who prescribed Prozac. After taking the medication for a month, Adam was still talking about wanting to die. At that point, his psychiatrist told Bob and Lisa that he should be hospitalized for his own safety.

"Adam has disliked school ever since fourth grade," Bob said. "But for the past few months, he has refused to go to school at all. He's been staying home and becoming more and more depressed. He has an independent study contract with the high school, but he only does the bare minimum."

"What grade is Adam in?" I asked.

"He's in ninth grade," Lisa said. She seemed very sad and worried.

I asked the couple about their marriage, and they said they were happy together. Their only source of unhappiness was Adam. He was going downhill rapidly after almost a year of therapy. Their other children were testing limits by not doing their chores, but they were good kids. "We're just mystified as to why Adam is so unhappy," Lisa said.

"Does the Prozac seem to be helping him?" I asked.

"Maybe a little," Bob said. "But even in the hospital he's been talking about wanting to die."

At the end of the session, I told them that I would like the whole family to come to the next session. "Now that I've met you, I would like to talk with your three children together."

My thinking was that I would get more information about the source of Adam's problem by meeting with him and his siblings alone. In fact, seeing just the kids is one of my most useful therapeutic tools. Siblings tend to be much more revealing, and less inhibited, when they meet with me without their parents.

At the next session, Lisa and Bob introduced their children to me, and I invited them into my office. Jason and Brenda took a seat on the sofa, while Adam slouched across the love seat. He was dressed in dark denim jeans with a black hooded sweatshirt pulled down over his eyes.

"So," I asked them, "what's the problem?"

"I'm the problem," Adam volunteered from under his hood.

"Why is that?" I asked.

"Because I want to die," he replied.

"I see. Well, are there any other problems in your family?"

"My dad works too much," chimed in Jason after a pause. "He just works and rides his bike. But mostly he just works, works, works."

"Do you think your dad works too much?" I asked, looking over at Adam, now slouched even further into the love seat.

"I want to die," Adam said unhelpfully.

"Who's the boss in your family?" I asked.

"I am," said Adam with no hesitation.

"Yeah," said Brenda. "He's the boss."

"So you kids run the ship?"

"Yeah, *we* run the ship. And I'm the captain," said Adam.

I looked at Jason, "And you're the first mate?"

"I guess so." Meanwhile, Adam had retreated deeper into his hood.

"How come your parents don't run the ship?" I asked.

"Because they never want to deal with anything," Adam said. "I just watch TV all day long and my father doesn't do anything about it."

"Shouldn't you be doing your schoolwork?"

"Yeah, but my father just leaves me alone if I yell at him to stop nagging me. He doesn't make me do my work," Adam told me. Clearly, the hierarchy in this family was upside down. The parents had abdicated their role as heads of the family. Like many parents dealing with a depressed teenager who won't do his schoolwork, Lisa and Bob were feeling exhausted and defeated. I would need to strengthen and energize the parent subsystem, and get the parents to make sure Adam did his work.

"Well, do your parents go out alone sometimes, like on a date?" I asked.

Adam answered, "No. My dad has poker night on Wednesdays, but they never go out together anymore. They're always too tired."

"Are you more worried about your mother or your father?" I asked them. They all agreed that they were more worried about their father because he worked so much and seemed depressed at times. They also told me that their grandfather, their father's father, had begun to have symptoms of Parkinson's disease, and their parents were very worried about him. Adam told me that he sometimes went over to his grandfather's house to help him with chores and errands.

"So, you're the family helper," I said to Adam.

"Yeah, I guess so," he mumbled.

"Maybe I can take over that role now. I could be your family's helper instead of you. That's my job, you know, helping parents and helping kids." Adam slouched into his hood. But he did look at me a little more attentively with his intelligent brown eyes. I thought it was time to bring Lisa and Bob into the session. When they came in, Lisa sat between Brenda and Jason on the couch. But with Adam slouched across the love seat, there was no place for his father to sit.

"Could you bring in a chair from the waiting room for your father?" I asked Adam, beckoning him with my hand. Surprisingly, this oppositional, depressed young man instantly sprang up, went out to the waiting room, and brought a chair into the office. I asked him to place the chair right next to me, and invited Bob to sit down. Bob was now in an elevated position in the room, sitting next to me like a co-therapist. Adam sat up a little straighter; no sign of the slouch now. He was responding well to an adult taking charge of the situation. So often, troubled teenagers are looking for firm limits and parental authority. Adam was not disengaged from his family, as many teenagers are today in their peer-dominated, hierarchy-less subculture. Instead, he was *overly* engaged with his parents and overly worried about them.

I asked Adam to give his parents some advice on how to be happier. Here I was using the reversed hierarchy in a productive way, putting Adam in charge of his parents' happiness. He rose to the task, suggesting that his parents go on bike rides together instead of his father riding his bike alone all the time. He also said that they should go out to dinner together like they used to do, and go to more events at their temple. Meanwhile, Adam had taken down his hood and was looking more alert and attentive to what was going on in the session.

My hypothesis was that Adam had been feeling worried about his father and was staying home from school to keep him company. Staying home also allowed him to go to his grandfather's house during the day and help him out.

I met with Lisa and Bob over the next few months. Like many couples who had been married for two decades, Lisa and Bob had simply drifted apart, with their energies focused on their children's activities and their time-consuming jobs. There were no deep-seated resentments between them. I helped them agree on some rules around Adam's schoolwork, and they decided to keep the TV cable unplugged until Adam showed Bob that he had completed his assignments for the day. They would also monitor Adam's computer use, allowing him to be online only for school assignments. Bob, who described himself as more passive than his wife and more laissez-faire about discipline, promised to monitor Adam's schoolwork more closely. Like many parents who fear being too authoritarian with their kids, Bob had all but abdicated the leadership that Adam badly needed. Lisa admitted to being controlling and overinvolved with Adam's problems, and said she would back off and let Bob take charge of Adam.

I also met with Adam individually for a few sessions. At first, like most teenagers, he tenaciously resisted his parent's discipline regime, grumbling when his father disconnected the TV cable or made him take out the garbage. But in time Adam felt relieved when he saw his parents working together and taking charge of him and his siblings. Adam also told me that his parents were going out more and seemed a little happier. When the new school year started, Adam went back to attending school. Under his psychiatrist's supervision, he gradually stopped taking the Prozac.

Author and therapist Ron Taffel argues that today's teens are "vertically challenged," living increasingly in the media-dominated world of their peers rather than in a stable, predictable family that has dinner together every night. Because of this cultural shift, Taffel believes that therapists need to reexamine yesteryear's notion of healthy parental boundaries and family hierarchy. Yet, in his opinion, kids still yearn for "engagement" with their parents, albeit engagement on their own terms.

This means that parents must catch their teen between tweets, texts, e-mails, phone calls, and instant messages to their friends. Parents must also tune in to their teen's "conversational style." If the teen is an active learner who hates to stop moving, for example, parents need to state rules while their teen is engaged in another activity. Other teens need explicit, unambiguous statements of rules in circumstances where they have their parent's full attention. Whatever their style of interaction, however, teens today are not so unlike previous generations—in that clear rules and boundaries provide a predictable environment in which they feel safe.

Despite the frenetic pace of today's teenagers, I would argue that some teens, at least, still worry about their parents, and this is what causes them to have problems. They may worry even more than in previous generations because parents today are confronted with more stresses in a fragmented and fragmenting culture. A sixteen-year-old client told Taffel that she thought her parents were unhappy because they hated their jobs, hated their marriage, and hated just about everything in their lives. In my view, this suggests that teens will feel better when they hear more positive than negative remarks from their parents about their own lives and when they see their parents holding hands and smiling as they cheerfully walk out the door for a date.

Today's teens may be more technologically savvy and more connected to a vertical peer culture than previous generations. But I have found that therapy is still most productive when the therapist views a teenager's symptoms as helpful to one or both parents. This doesn't mean, though, that therapists can ignore other factors involved in teen problems, like their relationships with peers, their conversational style, and even their temperament.

In our culture, adolescence stretches out longer than ever before, with young people in their twenties often moving back to the parental nest—if they ever left it at all. In the next chapter I look at the twenty-somethings who linger betwixt and between adolescence and adulthood—often with troubling consequences.

EIGHT

Threshold Kids

A Passage in Search of a Rite

THE STAGE IN FAMILY LIFE when a son or daughter moves away from home can be the best of times or the worst of times. Some young people easily navigate the first passage out, never moving back home once they leave. They travel along a smooth path from home to college and then to graduate school or work, living on their own successfully. They visit their parents for holidays, and may ask for an occasional loan to tide them over; but these kids have, in their own and their parents' views, successfully "left home." This does not mean that they will not want to return to the safe harbor of their parents' homes once in a while. They simply want the independence to pursue their own goals and dreams without interference. They still love their parents and count on them for emotional support. At the same time they are determined to make their own decisions, and need their parents to respect their boundaries.

But what about the young people who get caught in a revolving door, moving in and out of their parents' house multiple times as they struggle to embark on their journey to adulthood? For them, the transition across the threshold into the wider world of work or school and new relationships can be perilous and fraught with difficulty for the whole family. Some threshold kids live at home because of emotional problems. They flunk out of college, have difficult breakups with lovers, or cannot support themselves. These kids collapse back home and expect to live there more or less indefinitely as if they were still adolescents. They lack the motivation and drive to look for work, and they often become apathetic or even depressed, spending their days watching television or playing video games. Some of these kids use drugs or get into trouble with the law. They become stuck on the threshold, unable to move out into the world of adult responsibilities, yet are unhappy with being treated like a child at home. Some of them develop chronic problems and eventually become labeled "mentally ill."

And what of the young people who move back home in their twenties and even their early thirties because they lose their jobs or can't find jobs after college or graduate school? In these financially perilous times, a "boomerang kid" or a "bungee family" doesn't always suggest a young adult with chronic emotional problems. Indeed, in many countries—including Italy, much of the Middle East, and South America—it is the norm for a young person to live with his or her parents until marriage. This is not to say that parents and their emotionally healthy threshold kids don't get on one another's nerves. Mothers and fathers who have grown accustomed to a peaceful empty nest are appalled to see clothes and shoes littering their tidy home and are annoyed to hear rap music booming from their kid's room. Parents constantly second-guess themselves: "Should we be putting up with Heather coming home at three in the morning?" or "Should we demand that Frank wear headphones so we don't have to listen to his music?"

Parents and offspring have to renegotiate their relationship to minimize emotional tension and stress. In time they learn to adjust their expectations, eventually interacting more like roommates than like parents and children, with shared household responsibilities and mutual agreements about decibel levels. The best chance of success comes when parents are explicit about what they will or will not tolerate. Drawing a parental bottom line, though it may seem like a hardship for the kid, is paradoxically just what it takes for these young people to become a tad more mature. A little hardship is not a bad thing to help a young person grow up.

I know a young woman, Allison, who moved back to her parents' suburban home with her husband and infant daughter after her husband lost his job. Allison's father, Gary, was not happy with this situation, as he had never liked his son-in-law. Every time Gary came home from work and drove up their driveway, he felt so tense that his stomach clenched. He had to sit in his car for a few minutes to prepare himself to walk into the house and see his son-in-law.

Allison's mother, Hannah, felt the same way about the man her daughter had married. In fact, when Allison announced that she and Jonah were engaged, Hannah's jaw literally dropped. However, despite how upset she was about the live-in situation, she was able to keep quiet about it for her daughter's sake. She kept reminding herself of her grandmother's advice: "Bite your tongue until it bleeds and then keep biting."

Gary and Hannah gave the young couple occasional gifts of money and bought clothing and other necessities for their granddaughter; but they made it clear that this was not a permanent handout or an ongoing living situation. They remained friendly and reassuring— and went on with their own lives. Fortunately, Hannah and Gary had a supportive group of friends who listened to their complaints and sympathized with them. And the couple also came to see me in therapy on occasions when the situation threatened to get out of control.

I was usually able to calm them down and suggest strategies—in addition to Hannah's grandmother's good advice—for handling what was intrinsically a stressful state of affairs. Finally, after a year and a half, Allison's husband found a job in a town about an hour away, and the young couple was able to afford a place of their own.

Gary and Hannah were fortunate. Their daughter was happy with the man she married—even though they weren't—and she and Jonah managed to be pleasant enough to her parents while living in their home. Other parents are not so lucky. A couple I saw for marital therapy had become so distraught about the intrusion of their son, his wife, and their three-year-old twins that the two families became locked in a daily battle about such issues as clutter and who would buy the groceries and do the cooking. Every day the parents came home from work to find dirty dishes piled up in the sink and clothing and toys strewn all over the house. Neither their daughter-in-law nor their son had begun preparations for dinner. The parents told me that they felt like they were living under a "cloud of misery" and didn't know what to do.

I counseled them to spend as much time as possible away from home, going out with friends and doing volunteer work at their church. I also suggested that they make the rules of their home explicit to their son and daughter-in-law, and make it very clear that infractions of the rules would mean that they had to move out. They gave the young couple one chance after another to cooperate. Finally, the parents reluctantly sold their house and moved into a small town house. They gave their son money for the first and last month's rent in an apartment, but he became so angry that he now refuses to speak to his parents at all.

In our society there is no socially sanctioned right way for young-sters to move out of their parents' homes and make the transition to adulthood. For the most part, families and kids navigate this life stage alone, without the benefit of guidance from social traditions and institutions. This may be more of a misfortune—both at the individual and the societal level—than we realize.

Unlike modern society, most "traditional" cultures, such as the Masai of Kenya, acknowledge that the passage from adolescence to adulthood is a painful and perilous life crisis, and they have elaborate rituals to guide young people safely through the transition. These rites of passage always include a ceremony for crossing the threshold, or *limen* (the Latin word for threshold). After they have separated from their families, the young initiates live communally (boys separate from girls) for a specified period of time, with particular foods, clothing, and symbols to demarcate their status as *liminals*. The young initiates have to undergo certain ritually prescribed hardships, which may include mutilations, whippings, piercings, and tattoos. During this time, they live in a geographical no-man's-land, apart from the rest of the community, signifying that they have not yet assumed a place in adult society.

Only by enduring both the prescribed physical hardships and the sadness of separating from their parents can the young people become integrated into the community as adults. At this point they are deemed ready to take on new and well-defined social roles, and can never return to being children in their parents' homes. The novices learn to live differently from the way they lived in childhood. This transition to adulthood is guided by trusted older members of the community, who have a semi-magical status as participants in the ritual.

Family physician and research psychologist Leonard Sax laments the lack of such traditions in our own society and warns of the grave consequences for individuals, families, and society. In his fascinating book *Boys Adrift*, Sax points to our culture's neglect of rites of passage as the reason that so many young men in our society remain stuck in adolescence. And, argues Sax, our collective disregard for rites of passage has even more serious consequences than merely "failure to launch." If boys do not have good role models in the community to help them become men, gang rituals and street violence may take the place of socially sanctioned and regulated initiations. Sax goes on to warn us that we "will learn the hard way why traditional cultures invest this tradition with so much importance."

Sax offers excellent suggestions for helping boys move into responsible manhood. Boys' clubs like the Boy Scouts, all-male retreats in churches and synagogues, and single-sex schools and colleges can all supply good role models. Although Sax has chosen to write about boys, he acknowledges that the transition to adulthood can be difficult for girls in our society as well. And thinkers from Simone de Beauvoir to Mary Pipher have lamented the absence of rituals and role models to help young females successfully navigate the transition from girlhood to womanhood without losing their best qualities in the process.

Our secularized society has few rituals to help young people make the transition to adulthood. Religious ceremonies such as confirmation, bar mitzvah, and bat mitzvah mark the transition to physiological adulthood and once symbolized adolescents' readiness to marry. But in modern society, after these rituals are over the young person continues to live in his parents' home as an adolescent.

In fact, our society blurs the line between adolescence and adulthood. True social adulthood, with its many responsibilities and privileges, has become successively delayed. Going away to college may seem like a rite of passage. But the young person in a dorm—who has his meals served to him and his bills paid by his parents—has not by any stretch of the imagination left childhood behind. Moreover, the college student, unlike Thomas Wolfe, knows that he *can* go home again—during school vacations and even after graduation from college—and resume his childhood role, with his mother doing his laundry and cooking his meals, and his father giving him an allowance. Graduation from college, though it is a passage of sorts, does not in itself guarantee that a young person will be ready to get a job, find a place to live, and take on the weighty social burdens of adulthood. The comforts of the nest are often more appealing than striking out on one's own.

Sometimes it is the parents who have difficulty letting go of their nestling. I have seen parents try to control their son or daughter's choice of college or career, just as they chose their child's elementary school or high school. Parents who have played a large role in the school years—volunteering in the classroom, chaperoning field trips, intervening in the choice of teachers—may find it especially difficult to back away from their adult child's decision making. I have met parents who have been so intensely involved in parenting that they linger in a state of denial or grief at the prospect of their child's leaving home and making his own decisions about his future. These parental stances are not without consequences. As a family therapist, I see many young people who become depressed or angry or moody when their parents, usually for the most benevolent of reasons, interfere with their natural process of growth and development.

Several years ago I treated a family in which the seventeen-year-old daughter, Iris, an honor student in her senior year of high school, was having angry outbursts over trivial issues. Her explosions alternated with bouts of sadness, during which she would lock herself in her room, weep, and refuse to talk to her parents for hours or even days.

Iris's parents were frightened by the abrupt change in their daughter's personality. Iris had always been the "perfect" daughter, making her parents proud. Before she consulted me, Iris's mother had become alarmed by a magazine article that identified abrupt mood swings in teenagers as a sign of bipolar disorder. When she called me, she told me that she and her husband were worried that Iris might need medication.

Iris's parents, Arjun and Iksha, came from India, where they had been trained as physicians. When they moved to California, they found the requirements for licensing so demanding and expensive that they reluctantly gave up their dreams of practicing medicine in the United States. Instead, they each took university research positions with which they were able to support their family as well as their elderly parents in India.

Iris had told her parents she wanted to speak with me privately, but she agreed to let them accompany her to the first session. After our introductions in the waiting room, Iris followed me into my office. To put her at ease, I began by asking her about her activities and her classes. I learned that she was on the school swim team and was taking all honors and advanced placement (AP) classes. Her favorite subject was creative writing. After a few minutes, she was comfortable enough to open up about what was making her so miserable.

"Since I was seven," she said, "I've known that my parents expected me to study medicine. They made no secret of that—and I know why. But," and here she hesitated, not sure how I would react, "I really want to study literature and teach college classes some day. I don't know how to say this to my parents without hurting them."

Compliant with her parents' wishes for most of her life, Iris was now feeling the pull of her own passions. Desperate to make her own decisions about her future, she was painfully conflicted.

"I know that studying literature is impractical," she admitted. "I would make a much better living—and probably have more prestige—as a doctor." She shook her head as if to banish the thought. "And I *could* go to medical school if I wanted to. I'm really good at chemistry and biology. I take AP classes in both subjects." With these last words, her voice quivered. She was close to tears. Then she added, "But I just don't want to take so many science classes. I really want to study literature."

She looked over at me, anxiously waiting to see how I would respond.

"I think your parents would want you to be happy," I said promptly. I knew I was going out on a limb in assuming that Arjun and Iksha could be rational about this matter.

"That's what they tell me too. But . . . ," she hesitated, "at *another level* I sense that they would be really disappointed in me if I didn't study medicine."

On the one hand, Iris wanted to please her parents and comply with their unspoken but deafeningly loud wish that she become a doctor, thus fulfilling their thwarted hopes for themselves. On the other hand, she did not want to go through the rigors of medical school simply to fulfill her parents' dreams. But standing up to her parents was difficult for her. She knew that her parents had sacrificed a great deal so that she would have more opportunities. She felt torn, and that in turn was making her agitated and depressed.

In sessions with the parents and with Iris, together and separately, I was able to support Iris's wishes and help her parents reconcile their own conflict about her decision. I gave Iris the advice I often give young people who are caught between their parents' dreams for them and their own goals. I said: "Iris, your parents have made their own decisions, and they have to accept the consequences of those decisions. They have lived the lives they wanted to live. Now it's your turn to make your own choices and live your life as fully as you can."

Speaking privately to Iris's parents—with her permission—I explained that I thought Iris's mood swings and mental distress came from the pressure she was feeling about what to study at college, and about her conflict between pleasing them and pleasing herself. I acknowledged that they, too, might feel conflicted. They hoped their daughter would become a doctor and at the same time they knew the choice would have to be hers.

"I think you have to let Iris pursue her own dreams, not yours," I told them. "I think she knows that deep down you would be disappointed if she didn't study medicine, and this is causing her anguish."

I wondered if I was being too abrupt. Arjun and Iksha were sweet, sensitive people, and I found telling them the truth difficult, as did Iris. I didn't want them to feel blamed, nor did I want to take away their hopes. It would have been easier for me if they were not so appealing, but they had to hear this. Like many parents with children this age, Arjun and Iksha were having a hard time letting their daughter grow up and make her own decisions. They were afraid she would regret not studying medicine when she found out how difficult academic life could be. With a degree in medicine, they reasoned, she would always be able to have a good job. They wanted only the best for her. But their benevolence and overprotectiveness—appropriate when their daughter was younger—were unfortunately holding Iris back from her next developmental stage.

In the end, with my sympathetic coaching, Arjun and Iksha were able to give Iris a single, clear message that they wanted her to study whatever would make her happy. They saw how conflicted and unhappy she was while they still nurtured the hope that she would become a doctor. And, to their credit, Iris's parents were able to let go. At the last session with the three of them, Iris said that she finally felt that her parents were being sincere about allowing her to make her own choices. Shortly after this session, her moodiness disappeared and she became her old happy self. After graduating high school, Iris went off to college in the San Francisco Bay Area, where she majored in French literature.

Family therapist Milton Erickson observed that during the leaving-home stage of family life, the most destructive thing that parents can do is to be overindulgent and protective. Parental overprotectiveness without limits and consequences can make a young person incapable of moving on, and can keep a threshold kid in the gravitational orbit of his parents for an unhealthily long time. Even worse is a situation in which one parent is overly indulgent and the other is stricter and less sympathetic.

This was the circumstance in one of Erickson's cases in which a high school student was locked in an overprotective relationship with his father. The father, a physician, could not give up his indulgent way of parenting his son. No matter how offensively the young man behaved—ripping up his mother's clothes, using four-letter words at dinner, and being sexually explicit in front of his mother—his father would not draw the line and give him consequences. The mother, realizing that overprotectiveness had not served their son well, begged her husband to crack down on their son, but to no avail.

Erickson worked with the boy for several weeks, seeing him for an hour every day while his parents were away on vacation. Although Erickson made progress while he worked with him alone—motivating him to read several books, find an apartment, and think about getting a job—when the parents returned the boy quickly reverted to his outrageous behavior. At this point, Erickson told the parents candidly that he did not see any hope for their son, but he saw hope for the parents if they learned from this experience to treat their two younger children with less indulgence. One can scarcely imagine how painful it was for these parents to hear from a world-renowned therapist that there was no hope for their son. But Erickson said it this way because the parents needed to learn a hard and painful lesson. They needed to let go of their kids and allow them to grow up. Finally, these kindly parents took Erickson's advice—albeit harsh—with the result that their two younger children were able to develop normally.

As for the boy, he became so disturbed and disturbing to his parents—Erickson does not tell us exactly what he did—that they finally had him committed to a state mental hospital. He eventually was discharged; he called Erickson but never followed through on seeing him, to Erickson's deep disappointment. Erickson reflects, "He had the satisfaction of giving me the hope of seeing him, and I never heard from him again." This is an extraordinary comment from a doctor, to talk about hope and hopelessness. One feels that

Erickson was almost too sympathetic with this family. Commenting on the case, Jay Haley ponders why Erickson did not deal with the role that the boy's problem behavior had in the family system. He suggests that it was probably because Erickson was usually successful in disengaging a young person from his family by working with the kid individually.

I once saw a family similar in some ways to the one Erickson describes. In this family, the mother was overly lenient and the father was overly strict. The twenty-three-year-old son, Jonathon, still lived at home because he was too "depressed" to attend college or go to work. The only requirement his parents imposed was that he attend weekly individual therapy sessions with a psychologist and monthly sessions with a psychiatrist to monitor his medications. Jonathon spent the rest of his time at home playing video games and watching television. Every attempt his parents made to get him out the door failed because his mother could not entertain the possibility that her son might have to live on the street or in his car until he could chart his own path.

Jonathon's parents were resigned to this arrangement, even though their son himself had told them that they should throw him out. I came to know the family when the mother consulted me for a few sessions of therapy. She was distressed about Jonathon and hoped I might help her find a way to inspire him to move on. But as with Erickson's case, it was too late. There was nothing I could do to get the mother to set firm limits and become less indulgent with her son. She lived in constant fear of his living on the streets or committing suicide—something he occasionally threatened.

These two cases are a testament to the extreme pain that families and therapists can encounter in the leaving-home crisis. In fact, Jay Haley admonishes therapists to persist with these families until the kid has safely moved out of the house or the therapist reaches the age of eighty-five—whichever comes first. Jay was an inveterate devotee of brief therapy, but he was able to recognize that therapy with a family in this kind of predicament is not always amenable to a short time frame.

In most families, a modicum of maturity makes it possible for a young adult to leave the nest without turmoil. Sometimes, though, the nestling wavers at the threshold, unable to let go of the parents. This doesn't necessarily mean that the young adult is afraid of striking out on his own. It can occur when the parents are having marital problems and the young person starts to worry that their marriage won't survive without him. Just when he is supposed to be forging an independent identity, the unfortunate youngster becomes anxious or depressed, or engages in bizarre or dangerous behaviors, to distract his parents from their own troubles. The young person is then at risk for developing serious and chronic problems of his own.

Haley urged family therapists to view symptomatic young people who became stalled on the threshold as "sacrificing" themselves in order to keep their family stable. This idea was as unusual in 1980—the year Haley's seminal work, *Leaving Home,* was published—as it is now. Haley was talking about a special kind of failure to launch typified by two factors: the young person perpetually fails at school, at work, or both, and he is unable to form close relationships outside his family.

Haley was of course arguing against the prevalent view that schizophrenia and other serious afflictions are either biological or rooted in the person's inner conflicts. He urged that the troubled kid, whom he preferred to call "mad" or "eccentric" rather than "ill," be viewed in the social environment in which his problem was generated—that is, the family undergoing a painful developmental crisis. He believed that the young person was distracting the parents from their own sorrows: the sadness of their youngster leaving home and their painful marital difficulties.

Haley also focused on the odd manner of communication that

these young eccentrics tend to use—that is, they often communicate metaphorically rather than directly. An example of this was Erickson's patient, whom we met in a previous chapter, who insisted that he was Jesus Christ, using the image of Jesus to communicate the depth of his suffering. Whether this mode of interacting is a defense that prevents the kid from feeling pain, or whether it serves some other purpose such as making the young person feel more in control, Haley did not specify. This was probably because he did not find explanations in terms of inner feelings useful for the purposes of therapy.

When parents start treating their anxious or depressed youngster more like a responsible adult and less like a dependent child, *and* when they convince the kid that they can do very well without him under their roof, the outcome is more positive. Parents must also convey to their son or daughter their confidence that he or she can do well in the wider world without *them*, while also offering reassurance that leaving the nest does not mean cutting off contact with the family.

Regardless of what parents do—reassuring their offspring, setting limits, reinforcing the child's moves toward maturity—if all is not well at the hearth, young adults may have problems breaking away. Haley describes an eighteen-year-old girl named Annabelle who was hospitalized for severe depression and drug use. Annabelle's parents had long-standing marital difficulties that were so severe that, during their arguments, her mother would threaten to leave her father. What held their marriage together was that they had to take care of their "sick" daughter.

The family therapist whom Haley was supervising had the difficult task of challenging the parents' overprotectiveness toward Annabelle, whom they pitied because they believed she was ill. In discussing the rules they would impose on Annabelle when she came home from the hospital, the parents focused mainly on what Annabelle would be comfortable with. To help them take control of the situation, the therapist had to insist that the point was not what rules their daughter would be more comfortable with but what rules would make *the parents* comfortable. The discussion of rules, however, was really a way of helping the parents come to agreement in their marriage—for that was the real focus of the therapy. As long as turmoil and conflict reigned in their relationship, Annabelle would not recover.

Once Annabelle was home and behaving normally, her parents threatened to separate. This of course verified Haley's hypothesis that Annabelle was trying to save her parents' marriage by having symptoms. The therapist privately secured an agreement from the parents that they would stay together at least until Annabelle graduated from high school. They respected the agreement, and soon after Annabelle graduated and moved to her own apartment, her mother left her father. By this time, Annabelle was working at a job she liked and had made some friends, and she continued to do well after her parents separated.

Haley emphasizes that parents taking charge of their troubled offspring is crucial in stabilizing the family. But often parents resist assuming authority. The family system opposes change and strives toward homeostasis, or stability, and from this perspective the problem child serves to stabilize the family. By the same token, the parents may feel unable to change because they are discouraged and worn down by the losing battles they have waged with their kid, and by their repeatedly failed attempts to take control.

Haley lists several ways that parents resist taking charge. They may refuse to accept the family therapist as an authority. This is what Paige's father did when he insisted that his sister, a psychiatrist, knew how to help Paige better than I did. Feeling overwhelmed and powerless, the parents may turn to outside experts like psychiatrists or the police. Because they feel so out of control, they may even entrust their youngster to a residential treatment facility. Often, parents may sabotage their own authority by turning on each other. Arguments may arise when one parent feels that the other is being too tough with the kid who is, after all, "ill," while the other parent feels that discipline is the key.

Yet another form of resistance is for the parents to recruit a relative, such as a grandparent, who attempts to take charge of the therapy. For example, the mother of a troubled teen whom I had been seeing in family therapy told me that her own mother (the girl's grandmother) thought I should see the girl individually. The grandmother was a third-grade teacher with no training at all in therapy. To this I replied that the grandmother should call their pediatrician (with whom I was working closely on this case) and advise him on how to practice pediatrics. I heard no more about the grandmother, and the girl continued to improve in family therapy.

Countering these resistances—and putting parents firmly in charge of their offspring—is an essential first step in addressing the young person's crisis, no matter the circumstance. But it becomes especially crucial when the adolescent is suffering from anorexia or some other life-threatening disorder. Salvador Minuchin developed a unique strategy to get the parents of anorectic young women to take control of their eating. He usually used this strategy during a therapy session itself, which took place while the girl was in the hospital. Taking control sometimes meant that the parents, under Minuchin's guidance, had to physically put food into their daughter's mouth.

"What if we aren't able to keep our daughter safe and get her to gain weight when she comes home?" implored the anxious parents. When this happened, Minuchin spoke solemnly to the parents about the likelihood of their daughter dying or being rehospitalized. He reminded them that every time their daughter came home, she would still be their responsibility. Eventually, they would have no choice but to take charge and see to it that their daughter gained weight, so they might as well begin right away. This tactic usually worked. Minuchin helped parents come up with a concrete plan of how much weight their daughter would gain each week, which parent was to weigh her, and what she was going to eat each day.

Haley suggested the possibility that the often bizarre behaviors of young people—starving themselves, as Minuchin's patients did, getting in trouble with the law, abusing drugs, becoming severely depressed or anxious, or using language in strange ways—are most productively viewed as signs of a life crisis of the young adult and his family, rather than symptoms of a biological brain disorder. But, as we know, a more biological standpoint has held sway in recent years. In the last decade, research has revealed that the prefrontal cortex, the part of the brain responsible for complicated decision making, planning, and understanding the consequences of one's behavior, is not fully developed until after age twenty or so. Developmental psychologists and neuroscientists point out that teenagers behave irresponsibly, or what Haley would call "crazily," because their brains have not fully matured. An immature brain may interact with the crisis of moving into adulthood to produce impulsive and risky behaviors.

This is an intriguing explanation. But, as one mother of a risk-taking teen said to me when I cited the research, "That doesn't explain to me why most of the kids at my son's school are not screwing up the way he is. What about *their* immature prefrontal cortexes?" The answer is, of course, that our explanations have to be multitextured to encompass all the relevant dynamics—including biological, familial, and cultural or societal factors. Ultimately, every child is a unique blend of all of these influences. And because life experiences and relationships—friendships, romantic attachments, and associations with teachers, parents, and other adults—also play a part in shaping human development, we must look beyond a single biological factor to understand why some adolescents make bad decisions or have trouble leaving home and assuming adult roles.

As Haley suggested decades ago, in our culture family therapy can be a substitute for the social rituals that smooth the passage to adulthood in traditional societies. Working with a threshold kid and his family, a therapist can often help the young person become motivated to get a job, take college classes, and eventually move out of his parents' house to live on his own.

The idea of family therapy standing in for a traditional rite of passage is very much on my mind these days as I work with a sadly troubled twenty-two-year-old girl named Kati. In our second therapy session, Kati told me directly that she was tired of "helping her parents" by having problems. Kati was living with her parents, although she has been out of high school for four years. A pretty girl with a cap of blond curls, Kati is adorned with every imaginable type of body piercing and tattoo. Her toenails and fingernails are painted black, and she often wears black lipstick. Kati and her family came to see me after she had been hospitalized for cutting and depression.

In the course of therapy, I have found that Kati's parents have unwittingly sabotaged every step she's taken toward independence. Profoundly worried about their daughter, they feel they must help her in any way they can. So instead of expecting her to get a job and work even part-time, they pay for her car insurance, gas, and designer clothing. Unfortunately, this indulgence has been crippling for Kati.

Kati's father was critical of Kati all through her childhood and is critical even now, when she is in so much pain. She feels she can never please him. No matter how many A's and awards Kati got in school, he kept raising the bar, eroding her self-confidence. Now that she is out of school, her father never stops criticizing her appearance—the color of her hair, her clothing, her makeup—and especially her tattoos. He seems to have an image in his mind of a perfect daughter, Kati says ruefully, and she always falls short of the mark. Her mother is more accepting, but, says Kati, her mother is "under my father's thumb" and unhappy in their marriage.

After nine months of family therapy, we have made some progress. Kati moved out of her parents' home. She is living with her boyfriend in a nearby town and attending community college. Her parents are coming to me for marriage counseling and family counseling. I have been fairly successful in helping them make a life of their own that doesn't center on Kati. Recently, they drove to Arizona to see the Grand Canyon and spend a few days in Sedona. They stayed at a romantic little bed-and-breakfast. They both enjoyed the trip and feel that it revitalized their relationship. They hadn't taken a vacation alone together for many years. I don't know whether or not the parents will stay together, but at least now there is some hope for Kati. Still taking medication for depression, she plans to wean herself from it eventually with the help of her psychiatrist.

Not long ago Kati brought in a book, *The House on Mango Street*, which she is reading for her literature class. She told me that at the end of the book the author talks about someday leaving her mother's home, the house on Mango Street. Kati read: "She does not hold me with both arms. She sets me free. One day I will pack my bags of books and paper. I am too strong for her to keep me here forever."

Katie tells me she used to feel like that, "like my parents were holding me with both arms. I felt like I was imprisoned."

And so she was, I say to myself.

"Do you still feel that way?" I ask.

"No," says Kati, without hesitating. "Now I feel almost strong enough to pack my books and paper and write my own story."

Her words made me smile.

NINE

From Biology to Benevolence

OUR CHILDREN ARE IN TROUBLE today because our families are in trouble. I write this at the start of 2010. America's economic future is uncertain, and jobs are still being lost at an unprecedented rate. People who have played by the rules—worked hard, paid their bills, saved for their children's education—are losing their homes and often their hope. I am already seeing the toll this is taking on families

As more families lose their jobs and their homes, I worry about a worsening mental health crisis for our children. I expect that children will take on the task of distracting their parents from their painful losses, and will have even more profound troubles than they are having now. And if something does not change in the mind-set of our society, parents will continue to turn to pharmaceutical solutions for their children because drugs are the mainstream choice.

I am already starting to see a wave of children whose parents are breaking down under the stress of having their hours and salaries cut or losing their jobs altogether. These young people are desperately worried about their parents' fights over money. Recently a mother called me for an emergency weekend appointment after her eleven-year-old son, Drake, tried to hang himself from the post of his bunk bed. Earlier he had threatened to jump out of his bedroom window.

In my office, Drake's parents spoke frantically, between anxious tears, about depression and medication and hospitalization. Of course, I take any threat of suicide, even a symbolic one, very seriously, and I listened closely, pondering what the next step should be. Then, in a private conversation with Drake, he confessed to me that his feet were on the floor while he pretended to hang himself. He told me straight out that he just wanted his parents to stop arguing about money.

Drake was sad to the point of despair because his father had been laid off from his job and his parents didn't know if they would be able to keep their house. Drake's parents were responsible people and usually took care not to argue in front of their children. But these catastrophic issues loomed so large in their daily life that Drake couldn't help but know what was going on.

Despite the gravity of Drake's gesture and his parents' plight, I was able to help. I framed Drake's behavior as sadness—indeed, an appropriate emotion under the circumstances—and I explained to his parents that I thought Drake was unhappy and worried but not suffering from a psychiatric disorder. I encouraged his parents to reassure him realistically that they would be able to manage and were working together to come up with good solutions.

His mother said she would probably be able to increase her hours at the insurance company where she now worked part-time. And she thought her parents might be willing to help them with a short-term loan until her husband found another job. Drake's father, who had worked as a manager at an aerospace company, said he would look into taking classes that would enhance his resume. Drake's parents were very cooperative when I told them how important it was to keep their problems and arguments away from the children. After a few sessions of family therapy, Drake was back to normal.

But many parents are not as fortunate as Drake's, whose health insurance paid for family therapy and whom I was able to help without resorting to medication or hospitalization. In a society where so many mothers and fathers have reached the breaking point from stress and worry, a lot of parents embrace medication, for themselves and their children, because they are not aware of an alternative. The pendulum has swung very far in the direction of pharmaceutical cures, "cures" for what—as I've pointed out—are usually not "diseases" at all. It would have been all too easy to diagnose eleven-year-old Drake with depression or even bipolar disorder, and to recommend that a psychiatrist be consulted for medication. But this would not have eased the sadness and stress that were the real causes of his suffering.

Autism researcher Simon Baron-Cohen reminds us that the Diagnostic and Statistical Manual of Mental Disorders (DSM), with its shifting and changing content from edition to edition, is not a truly scientific classification system because it does not address the question of causes: "Psychiatry is not at the stage of other branches of medicine, where a diagnostic category depends on a known biological mechanism." Baron-Cohen points out that in the diagnosis of genuine medical disorders, such as Down syndrome, the biological cause of the abnormality—an extra copy of chromosome 21—is the specific basis for the diagnosis.

Psychiatric diagnoses, on the other hand, are more or less arbitrary clusters of symptoms that are given a name. These so-called disorders come and go with the times, with each new generation of psychiatrists deciding what the diagnostic categories will be in the newest version of the DSM. According to historian of psychiatry and author Edward Shorter, "In psychiatry no one knows the causes of anything, so classification can be driven by all sorts of factors"—political, social, and financial.

Certain diagnoses, such as bipolar disorder, have not been classified as childhood disorders in any version of the *DSM* since its inception in 1952. Yet more and more children are diagnosed each year with bipolar disorder. In branding children with this adult diagnosis, psychiatrists are not even abiding by their own manual of classification. This is a very slippery slope because, as we have seen, what looks like abnormal behavior in adults—such as impulsiveness, explosiveness, or believing in the tooth fairy—are perfectly normal behaviors in children. Even extreme mood swings or irritability, characteristic of bipolar disorder in adults, can be seen in normal children who may be reacting to family discord or other stressors in their lives. But giving a child the label of bipolar disorder can prevent that discord or stress from even coming to light and being addressed.

Gabrielle Carlson, director of child and adolescent psychiatry at Stony Brook School of Medicine, says, "Problematic conditions in a child's home life are less likely to be addressed if the child's behavioral issues are attributed to bipolar disorder. . . . Many people, when they hear bipolar disorder, their brains slam shut."

In a *New York Times Magazine* article (09/12/08) about childhood bipolar disorder, a psychiatrist gives two examples of what he considers manic behavior in a child: dressing outlandishly and talking to strangers. With this definition, we would have to diagnose Huckleberry Finn as manic (among other things), because Huck dressed in rags, avoided school, ran away from home, occasionally told lies, and freely talked to strangers. He would no doubt also be diagnosed with attention-deficit disorder because he hated school and with oppositional defiant disorder because he disobeyed one rule after another.

Huckleberry Finn, with his free spirit, his humor, and his ability to build warm friendships with the fascinating characters he meets along the river, was for many decades a boyhood hero for American youth. Huck symbolized freedom from the shackles of society and a spirit of adventure and self-reliance, along with a great capacity for empathy. But today, in our society, Huckleberry Finn would be diagnosable with several serious psychiatric conditions.

We must seriously ask ourselves where in the world of psychiatric diagnoses do "naughty," "mischievous," "headstrong," and "free-spirited" end and the diagnoses of manic, bipolar, and ADHD begin. There used to be some allowances in the way children were expected to behave, and some degree of consensus that childhood was a time for breaking rules, getting caught, being punished, and moving on. Teachers and parents alike recognized that normal children have a shorter attention span than adults. But today the *DSM* casts such a wide net that it would surely ensnare Huckleberry Finn, along with countless other "rascally" children.

What determines whether a condition finds its way into the *DSM*? The answer is more complex, and more disturbing, than one might expect. In meetings held over several years, diagnoses are hotly debated by the *DSM* panelists charged with creating each new edition; and these diagnoses are often politicized according to the temper of the times (not so long ago, homosexuality was considered a mental disease). The final decisions come down to the votes of these panelists.

This "classification by consensus" rather than by biological causes has been fiercely criticized by the media and by professionals, including some psychiatrists and psychologists. Yet this method of classification has prevailed, not the least because the panelists—the very doctors who decide how to name and classify psychiatric disorders—have powerful financial ties to the pharmaceutical industry. This industry, of course, stands to profit mightily from the insertion into the next *DSM* of pediatric bipolar disorder, or any other childhood psychological problem not previously classified as a disorder, and for which, conveniently, a drug treatment has been found to be effective at reducing symptoms.

Because of the heated debate about financial ties of *DSM* panelists, scientists who are working on the new *DSM-V* have agreed to limit their income from pharmaceutical companies and other sources to $10,000 a year for the duration of their work on the manual. This limitation does not extend to their accepting payments from pharmaceutical companies preceding or following their tenure as panelists. Some critics argue that this policy is not strict enough and that panelists should take no money at all from drug companies, to avoid conflicts of interest.

According to one study, 56 percent of the psychiatrists who wrote the *DSM-IV* had one or more financial links to a pharmaceutical company, and they did not have to disclose conflicts of interest. The *DSM* panelists are theoretically free to create new pathologies—for children or adults—in the service of the companies that finance them. Before 1980, for example, ADHD did not exist as a diagnosis. Then *DSM-III* panelists decided to give fidgetiness a medical name and deemed it a disorder—for which a drug treatment was readily available.

Now, *DSM-V* panel members working on childhood disorders are expected to hotly debate the merits of adding "pediatric bipolar disorder" as a distinct diagnosis. In my view, this addition would be tragic, as it would open the way for more children to be prescribed antipsychotic drugs for no sound medical reason. Even more troubling is the fact that children from low-income families, whose parents do not have private health insurance that covers family therapy or other counseling, would be drugged disproportionately. According to federally financed research by scientists at Columbia and Rutgers universities, children on Medicaid are given antipsychotic drugs at a rate four times higher than children whose parents have private insurance. And children on Medicaid receive the drugs for less severe conditions than middle-class children—for conditions such as ADHD or school conduct problems.

One fifteen-year-old New York girl on Medicaid was prescribed an antipsychotic drug after a single consultation, in which she was diagnosed with bipolar disorder. The doctor's diagnosis was based on the fact that she had arguments with her mother and stepfather and she suffered from insomnia. The girl decided to stop taking the antipsychotic because she discovered that she could control her moods without it. Nonetheless, she consulted another psychiatrist who accepted Medicaid to make sure she did not need the medication. After listening closely to the girl's story, this doctor told her that she was a normal teenager and did not need antipsychotic medication.

Medicaid provides antipsychotic drugs free of charge to covered children, at a cost of $7.9 billion as of 2006 (the most recent year for which data are available). Antipsychotics are the single biggest drug expenditure for Medicaid, and, surprisingly, they are sometimes prescribed by primary care physicians rather than psychiatrists.

As I've emphasized throughout this book, no matter how successful medication is in controlling children's behavioral symptoms, there are myriad downsides to kids taking psychiatric drugs. These range from immediate or delayed side effects of the medications (including cardiometabolic risks) to the drugs becoming a crutch and undermining a child's motivation to try to control his behavior and moods by himself.

Troublesome behaviors are not the only worry of today's parents. Mothers and fathers are also deeply concerned about their children's school performance. In a culture where the pressure on children to perform at peak levels is increasingly intense, I've heard otherwise sensible parents fret about their first-grader's chances of getting into Princeton or Harvard. Children are often forced into stressful situations over which they have no control. Indeed, some parents are so intent on their son or daughter succeeding academically that they forget about the child's uniqueness and aptitudes that are not measurable by standardized tests. These parents do not seem to notice that their child is empathic or generous or creative. They have little tolerance for their child's free-spiritedness. This attitude can have profound consequences.

In their willingness to use drugs to give their child a better chance of academic success, parents receive a lot of support in our society. By means of a psychiatric diagnosis and the latest designer drug, a child who is unruly or inattentive can be transformed into a well-behaved, studious child who will do his parents proud. An ADHD diagnosis means that a child will be allowed extra time on college entrance tests and in completing classroom assignments and exams. This will give him a better chance of doing well and being admitted to a good college or university. If he needs to take amphetamines to accomplish this, his parents reason that the end justifies the means.

But parents are often shortsighted when they think that entrance to an Ivy League university or a prestigious preschool will ensure their child's future success or happiness. Like swimming champion Michael Phelps, many children compensate for a weakness in one area by developing their talents in another. If a child focuses all his attention on keeping up academically, with academic success and admittance to an elite college as his only goal, he might never develop other unique aspects of his personality.

Sometimes parents have their heart set on a particular college or even a particular middle school or high school for their child— whether or not the child wants this for herself. This is what happened to a young girl I saw a few years ago. Eleven-year-old Shiloh came to therapy with her father, Larry, a widower who was raising his two children by himself after the death of his wife three years earlier. Larry sent Shiloh and her older brother to an exclusive private school that was regarded as the best in the community. He hoped that they would graduate from there and go on to a good college or university. He felt that he owed his late wife his best efforts to help Shiloh and her brother succeed in life.

But Shiloh had been getting D's and F's for more than a year at the new school, and Larry didn't know what to do. His daughter was bright enough to have been accepted by the school, and she had always been an "A" student in public school. He didn't understand why she was failing now. When Shiloh's teacher told him she thought Shiloh might have ADHD, Larry brought Shiloh to therapy hoping to get her back on track.

Shiloh confided to me that she hated the private school because the girls there were "really mean." They formed tight cliques and would gang up on one girl after another, gossiping and spreading nasty rumors. From one day to the next, Shiloh never knew who her friends were. Recently, two of her so-called friends had joined a clique of popular girls and turned against her.

With tears in her eyes, Shiloh told me that she just wanted to go to the public school in her neighborhood where she would be with the friends she had known since kindergarten. She was sure her old friends would be loyal to her, would never turn on her, and would never gossip about her behind her back or pick on her. She felt she could be herself with them and not have to put on an act in order to be accepted. I asked her if there were any mean girls at the public school, and if so wouldn't she have the same problem there. Shiloh thought about this. Then she replied that there were mean girls there, but she knew who they were and didn't count them among her friends. Shiloh promised she would get straight A's if her father sent her back to the neighborhood public school.

When I explained this to Larry, he was bitterly disappointed. He wanted his daughter to have all the advantages he never had. He had to go to work right after high school because his parents couldn't afford to send him to college. I told him that it would be easier for Shiloh to get into a good college with A's from a public school than with D's and F's from a private school, however exclusive.

"But doesn't she have ADHD?" Larry asked. I explained to him that I believed Shiloh's problem was not medical but situational. I thought she would do better in a different school—and especially a school where she wanted to go. If she continued to get bad grades there or if she demonstrated the typical symptoms of ADHD—distractibility, difficulty focusing on her schoolwork, or trouble sitting still—we could always reconsider. But, I added, I didn't think this would happen. Eventually Larry had to agree with me. Shiloh transferred to their neighborhood school and was much happier. Soon she was getting straight A's.

I do not dispute the fact that many adults have been helped by psychiatric medications, especially antidepressants. Antidepressants can help chronically depressed people function normally, and many seriously disturbed adults live normal lives thanks to medication. But children are another story. I have never seen a single child who could not be helped by family therapy if the child's parents were able to cooperate and follow my advice.

We must also keep in mind that there is an important ethical difference between prescribing psychiatric medications for adults and prescribing them for children. An adult can read and research the drug company's warnings and cautions. He can make an informed decision, weighing the benefits of the drug against the potential risks. A young child—even one old enough to read the words on the label—is not capable of understanding the message. (Adolescents, on the other hand, can understand the potential dangers of medication, and I've seen them refuse to take drugs that they think may harm them.) Although most parents are well intentioned, some can unwittingly medicate a child unnecessarily and can even increase the dosage to dangerous levels in order to keep their child under control.

The ethical responsibility of whether to trust a child's parents to use medications wisely is at present left to the conscience of the prescribing child psychiatrist. This means that the prescribing physician needs to accept more responsibility. She must be responsible for contacting other professionals involved with the child, such as pediatricians, teachers, therapists, and social workers. Unfortunately, the psychiatrist's medical training may not have prepared her for this responsibility, nor would she necessarily welcome this new obligation. The prescribing psychiatrist also has the responsibility of making sure that parents understand the labels on the drugs that warn of serious side effects, and that they understand the dangers of increasing dosages.

The drug industry has a huge stake in keeping psychiatrists prescribing their products for children—and understandably they do not emphasize either the side effects or the need for parental and medical vigilance. On the contrary, they are vigilant about denying any charges against them.

The pharmaceutical industry spends hundreds of millions of dollars a year on federal lobbying and has more than a thousand registered lobbyists. Our country's children who are being diagnosed and medicated with antipsychotics and other psychotropic drugs do not have a single lobbyist in Washington to protect their rights. They cannot organize and stand up for their own best interests. Human rights groups, such as the Nurses for Human Rights and the Council for the Human Rights of Children, feel that this inequity must be corrected. These health professionals maintain that policy makers have a responsibility to protect weak and vulnerable groups such as children. They believe that medicating a child with a psychotropic drug—except in the case of a biologically based illness—is a violation of a child's human right to security of person, a right that is spelled out in the United Nations 1948 *Declaration of Human Rights*. Many health professionals, from nurses to the family therapists and psychiatrists on the Council for the Human Rights of Children, believe that we cannot be value neutral in the face of violations of children's rights by psychiatrists, pharmaceutical companies, and insurance companies.

Apart from these groups, other doctors and therapists are becoming aware that there are ethical issues involved in medicating children. Pediatrician and family therapist Lawrence Diller, MD, points out that there is an ethical dilemma in giving a child a psychiatric drug because children "do not make the choice for themselves to take or not take a psychiatric drug."

These humanistic concerns make us mindful that there are weighty ethical questions involved with giving children psychiatric medications: the drug might cause the child harm or even death; the child cannot make an informed choice about taking the drug; drugs at best only mask the child's symptoms and do not solve the real problem in his life; and there are far safer and more effective solutions to the child's problems, such as the family therapy approach that I have described in this book.

The American Psychological Association recommends that non-drug treatment be considered first for childhood mental disorders. They suggest that professionals first try techniques that focus on parenting skills and that they enlist help from teachers and other school professionals before considering medication. According to a report in the *New York Times* (12/22/06), even the American Academy of Child and Adolescent Psychiatry, "an organization whose members favor drug treatment," recommends that "children receive some form of talk therapy before being given drugs for moderate depression."

Drug companies are not likely to change business practices that generate tremendous profits. But there are some encouraging signs that we are entering an era of increased accountability and transparency for institutions that receive public funding, such as medical schools, medical research centers, and federally funded health insurance programs such as Medicare. Senator Charles Grassley, the ranking member on the Senate Finance Committee, has tenaciously pursued what he views as improper conflicts of interest by psychiatrists conducting research on drugs that are approved for use by patients with Medicare and Medicaid. Grassley is working toward the passage of legislation that would require drug companies to publically report the money they give to doctors and medical researchers.

Fortunately, too, not all psychiatrists embrace the biological model, and a few are sounding the alarm. Chicago psychiatrist David Kaiser, MD, who is affiliated with Northwestern University Hospital, argues that for psychiatry to regain any semblance of legitimacy and integrity, "it must strip itself of false and hubristic claims and humbly submit itself to the urgent task of listening to individual patients with patience and intelligence." Dr. Kaiser finds it tragic that biological psychiatry has reduced patients to abstractions, "black boxes of biologic symptoms" that are disconnected from the patients' real life stories.

Increased accountability and transparency, along with the testimony of human rights groups and of psychiatrists like Dr. Kaiser, constitute the good news. But there is bad news as well. Child psychiatry continues to be dominated by a narrow medical approach. And much of the support for it comes from evidence that may be spurious or skewed. I have described in Chapter 1 some of the abuses of pharmaceutical companies, including concealing negative research results that put their products in a bad light. A recently revealed trend is the drug industry's practice of using company employees to "ghostwrite" articles in respected medical journals. The articles bear the names of doctors recruited by the drug company. According to University of Minnesota bioethicist Carl Elliott, this unethical practice has created "a huge body of medical literature that society can't trust."

This passionate debate between humanistic and biological views of human suffering is not new in the history of psychiatry. Philippe Pinel, a nineteenth-century French physician, is credited with being the first to release the mentally ill from their chains and treat them with talk therapy. Pinel believed that even severely disturbed patients could be helped by having a good relationship with a benevolent and compassionate human being. His therapeutic approach became known as "moral treatment."

Although moral treatment practitioners were originally medical doctors like Pinel, from the beginning they had a deep distrust for both organic explanations and pharmaceutical cures. They were more interested in the art of healing than in the medicaments of science. According to Robert Whitaker, author of *Mad in America*, one successful moral treatment asylum in the United States did not even allow physicians to sit on their board, "being fearful they might effect some innovation."

Social historian Michel Foucault tells us that the moral treatment cures of the nineteenth century were remarkably effective. Their effectiveness, Foucault argues, came from two essential elements of their practice that have all but disappeared in modern psychiatry: the therapeutic benefit of a good doctor-patient relationship, and the framing of even the most extreme forms of mental illness in the context of the patient's real-life experience. Loss of loved ones, financial ruin, poverty, betrayal by family and friends—all these misfortunes could transform human experience into forms of madness.

The remarkable successes of moral treatment came to an end in the late nineteenth century, when neurologists such as Charcot and Freud sought to make the cure of human suffering into a science. Doctors of the mind stopped listening to their patients' life stories and started attuning their ears instead to signs and symptoms of "disease." This led to another important and tragic transformation. Moral treatment therapists regarded their patients as moral equals. They took meals with their patients and strolled with them on the parklike grounds of the asylums. With the advent of "scientific" psychiatry, patients once again became morally inferior to their doctors.

The humanistic tradition of moral treatment, somewhat dormant during the rise of Freudian psychoanalysis, resurfaced in the middle of the twentieth century in the work of a few exceptional psychiatrists like family therapist Milton Erickson. Erickson, as we have seen, relied more on the curative power of a good therapist-patient relationship and on ordinary common sense than on the classification of human problems as mental illnesses. Like the moral treatment doctors a century before, he framed so-called psychiatric problems in relation to the patient's family life and social environment. In the same tradition, today's family therapists are taking more interest in the therapist-patient relationship, and they have a new concern with humanism and human rights.

Family therapists are mindful that the observer always influences the observed and, however elegant and effective our strategies may be, we must—as Foucault argued persuasively—make strong connections with our patients in order to help them. The therapist must be, as Pinel pointed out more than two hundred years ago, benevolent and compassionate. But she must also convey competence and authority. With children, the therapist must be gentle. Yet she must instill confidence in the child that she is capable of helping her parents, because that, in my view, is why the child is in the therapist's office—to get help for her parents. We must ask children questions that will draw them out, and we must pay close attention to their answers. As I have shown, children are the best experts on the difficulties in their families. The therapist must be humble enough to allow a child to be a co-therapist and guide her to the heart of the family's problem.

I am reminded of a six-year-old girl named Beth who, in the second family session, suddenly told me that her father was a doctor. She was letting me know that not only did I have to win *her* trust, I also had to win her father's trust in my behavioral approach to what he believed was his daughter's biologically based ADHD. I imagine Beth heard her parents discussing this issue at home and, quite rightly, she brought it to my attention in the session. As it turned out, her father was open-minded enough and cared enough about his daughter to give my program a fair try—with excellent results. After five weeks of family therapy, Beth's teacher said she was doing much better at school and stopped sending home notes about her misbehavior and slow academic progress. When it comes to their children, doctors are my best patients. They follow my directions to the letter because they trust professionalism.

The father of ten-year-old Brian was not a doctor, but, like Beth's parents, he trusted professionals and had an open mind. Brian and his family lived in Australia. Brian's father, Ron, was in Los Angeles on a business trip and had lunch with a former client of mine. When Ron talked about the problems his son was having, the client recommended me as a therapist who might be able to give him and his wife some ideas about how to help Brian. Ron called me immediately.

When we met, Ron told me that his son was desperately unhappy, and neither he nor his wife had any idea what was wrong or what might help him. Brian woke up every morning sad and teary eyed and refused to go to school. When his mother, Mary, tried to help him get ready for school, Brian threw himself on the floor and sobbed. This had been going on for six months. Mary took him to a child psychiatrist, who diagnosed him with depression and school phobia. The psychiatrist saw Brian once a week for talk therapy. But after six months there was little change in Brian's behavior or his sadness. Occasionally, Brian's mother could get him to walk with her to school. But soon the school would telephone and ask her to pick up her son because he was so miserable. The psychiatrist talked to the parents about starting Brian on antidepressants, but the parents were not happy with this solution.

"Brian has always been such a happy-go-lucky kid," said Ron. "His depression seemed to come from out of the blue. And I don't know why he would have school phobia all of a sudden. I mean, he's been in the same school for four years, and he always seemed to like it."

I said I thought I could help Brian if both Ron and his wife would follow the instructions that I would write down for them. On hearing this, Ron became upset. "It's something that I'm doing wrong. I knew it all along," he said. I reassured Ron that neither he nor his wife had done anything wrong. From what he had told me about their family, I could see they were terrific parents. I was just going to suggest different patterns of communication and behavior that had helped children with problems similar to his son's. Ron agreed to give my suggestions a try when he went back home to Australia. He felt they had nothing to lose since Brian's problems had not been resolved in six months of therapy, and seeing their son so unhappy was breaking their hearts.

Here are the directions I wrote down for Ron and his wife. (1) In the evening, after the children were in bed, they would make a list of Brian's positive qualities. Then every day, each parent would tell Brian five positive things about himself. (2) Every morning on the way to school, Mary would tell Brian why she was looking forward to her day. She had to be truthful, so she had to plan an enjoyable activity every day. When Mary picked up Brian from school, she was to tell him at least one thing that she had enjoyed during the day. (3) Ron was to spend a half hour every evening alone with Brian, either reading to him or helping him with his homework. Ron said that he could adjust his schedule by working a little from home later in the evening after the children were asleep. (4) During their evening time together, Ron would tell Brian at least one thing that he had enjoyed in the course of his day. (5) Neither parent was to yell at Brian or criticize him. They were to be patient and tender with him. (6) If the parents had disagreements with each other, they were to discuss them away from home, preferably in a restaurant. In fact, I asked them to schedule lunch or dinner out once a week to discuss Brian's improvement. Also, Ron and Mary were to take walks together in the evening to talk about Brian's positive qualities.

Finally, I asked that the parents contact me in six months to let me know how Brian was doing. They were to continue to do all these things until Brian's problems entirely disappeared. As for school attendance, I recommended that they let Brian go to school only when he was ready. They should expect him to go to school, and wake him up in time; but if he refused to go they should let him stay home. I didn't think it would take long for Brian to be back at school if his parents cooperated with me.

This was the first case I had ever conducted long distance, using only written instructions to the parents without ever meeting the child. I put Ron and Mary entirely in charge of their son's treatment. And I waited, with some trepidation, to see if Brian got better. My thinking was that Brian was protecting his mother and wanted to stay home from school to keep her company. He was worried about his mother's loneliness, with his father spending so many hours at work and traveling so often. My directives were aimed at releasing Brian from worrying about either of his parents and also involving father and son more so that Brian could disengage from his mother in a healthy way. I was also getting Brian's parents more involved with each other by asking them to spend more time together alone.

I did not hear from Ron and Mary for several months. Then one morning I received a letter from Mary. Here is what she wrote:

> At last I am writing to you. I'm sorry I haven't been in touch earlier to let you know how Brian is progressing. Until about two months ago I was still feeling a little on edge that his problem would return. However, touch wood, he seems to have resumed his old confident self.
>
> We followed your very valuable advice, which thoroughly intrigued Brian. He couldn't understand why we were being so nice to him. After a few weeks we started to see a marked difference and eventually the problem disappeared altogether. Now Brian is confident, loud,

naughty, cheeky and thoroughly objectionable—a return to the Brian we know and love! He is happy at school and getting good grades. So a big thank-you to you, Marilyn

I never stop learning from the families that consult me. Brian and his parents gave me two precious gifts: first, the realization that I could help a child entirely through his parents without ever seeing him; and second, a wonderful description of a ten-year-old boy as "naughty, loud, cheeky and thoroughly objectionable." What a refreshing picture of a healthy, happy boy!

How to Find a Family Therapist

ANY PEOPLE HAVE ASKED ME to provide guidelines for how parents can find a good family therapist. Just as you would take time to become an informed consumer before buying a new car or a new computer, you will need to put some time and effort into choosing the right therapist for your family. And the time you put in will be well spent.

A good place to start is with your pediatrician if she is open-minded about non-drug treatment of childhood problems. Ask if she can recommend a family therapist who has been successful in treating problems like the one your child is having. Word of mouth is one of the best ways to find a good therapist. Besides your pediatrician or family doctor, ask other people whom you trust for recommendations. Many people have had good experiences with family therapists and will likely be glad to pass on the therapist's name. Your child's teacher or school counselor may be able to give you a recommendation as well.

Your health insurance company may be another good source. Call the behavioral health division and ask a care manager to recommend an experienced family therapist in your area who specializes in children's problems. Get names from as many sources as possible, and look for therapists who get favorable comments from more than one source.

You want a therapist who identifies herself as a family therapist, whether or not she is specifically licensed as a marriage and family therapist (MFT). While some licensed marriage and family therapists have had training in family systems theory in their graduate degree programs, many have not. Some psychologists and clinical social workers may have pursued advanced training in family therapy, and identify themselves as family therapists.

Many therapists have Web sites where you can read about their training and their particular approach to children's problems. Look for someone who has made a specialty of working with families and children from a family systems point of view.

When you have a few names, I suggest that you ask the following seven questions, which I have devised to help parents become informed consumers. Therapists should be willing to answer at least two or three of these questions in an initial phone conversation. You may have to schedule a brief introductory session to get answers to all of them.

1. *How long have you been in practice as a family therapist?* Look for someone who has been practicing as a family therapist for at least five years.
2. *Do you ever see children and parents together in the same room?* The answer to this should be "yes."
3. *Have you successfully treated children with the type of problem my child is having? What is your success rate with this kind of problem?* Ask the therapist to be specific.

4. *Do you approach children's problems from a family systems point of view? If so, did you have supervision or training in this approach specifically?* The answer to these questions should optimally be "yes." If the therapist has had supervision at a family therapy training institute, this is a plus. If at all possible, find a therapist who has supplemented her academic training with postgraduate private training in family therapy by attending workshops, seminars, or conferences conducted by master family therapists.

5. *Do you see a child's problem as an individual problem or a social context problem?* The answer should be that the therapist takes the social context or interpersonal environment of the child into account.

6. *Do you ever consult with a child's teacher, school counselor, or other family members?* The answer to this question should be "yes." The therapist should be willing to talk with anyone in the child's social environment if she thinks it will help. Of course, the therapist will need to have your written consent to talk with anyone else about your child.

7. *How soon will I see improvement in my child?* Of course, it's difficult to predict exactly how many sessions it will take to see improvement, especially if the child has had a problem for a long time. But with a competent therapist, you should expect to see some minimal improvement after four or five sessions of family therapy.

It's important, too, that you feel comfortable with the therapist as a person. Does she listen carefully to what you say? Does he offer good suggestions or helpful behavioral techniques? Is she confident that she can help your family, or is she hesitant and unsure? Does the therapist seem like a caring person?

If a therapist talks about a "diagnosis" for your child in your initial conversation or in the first session, this is a red flag. You do not want a therapist who is interested in diagnosing or labeling your child and finding more symptoms that warrant that label. You want someone who will do what it takes to solve your child's problem. You also want a therapist who actively talks to you and offers good advice or concrete techniques to help your child, not someone who sits back and passively listens.

If you live in a small town or rural area, you might need to travel some distance to consult the right family therapist for your family, and have biweekly or monthly sessions. If your budget is limited, try to find a family therapy training program at a private training institute or at a college or university. These types of programs usually have low-fee clinics where student therapists are supervised by faculty. Some public health agencies, such as mental health centers, offer free or low-fee counseling. Many mental health centers have incorporated training in the family systems approach for the students and interns who work there. One of the best family therapists I know works at a public mental health center.

Finally, I hope you will consult my Web site—www.sufferthechildren .net, where you will find additional resources for parents.

ACKNOWLEDGMENTS

I THANK MY LITERARY AGENT, Susan Lee Cohen, who nurtured this project from its earliest beginnings and saw it through to the end with sensitivity, grace, and wisdom.

I have been fortunate in having exceptionally inspiring teachers along the road to becoming a therapist. I am grateful to Jarl Dyrud, MD, my dissertation advisor at the University of Chicago and my friend. In our meetings over the course of several years, Dr. Dyrud shared with me his wisdom, his wide experience, and his unique brand of humanistic psychiatry. Thanks also go to my supervisor and mentor Jay Haley, who, more than anyone else, taught me the art of family therapy.

I thank my supportive colleagues who have helped me in many different ways while I was writing this book: Chad Hybarger, Mike Robbins, and Lisa Harris.

I thank Maria Guarnascelli, my editor at Norton, for believing in this project from the outset and for her wise and invaluable contributions to the manuscript. She settled for nothing short of my very best, and I am deeply grateful to her for her persistence. Thanks also to Melanie Tortoroli at Norton for her gracious help with myriad details and her wonderful communication skills. Thanks go to Barbara Feller-Roth for her meticulous and intelligent copyediting.

My profound gratitude goes to Jo Ann Miller, editor extraordinaire, for seeing the statue in the marble and for helping me sculpt an unwieldy manuscript into a book.

I thank my husband, Gene, for his endless support and nurturing, and for putting up so gracefully and patiently with a writer-wife. He read and reread many parts of the manuscript, and his comments were always helpful. I thank my daughter Jessica for her assistance with the references and notes. Thanks also to Dan, Ellie, Theo, Jay, and Hayley for bringing us joy.

Most of all, I thank the clients with whom I have been privileged to work these many years and whom I cannot name. What I have learned has come mainly from them.

NOTES

INTRODUCTION: DO NO HARM

4   *doctors were beginning to question the very sanity*: See, for example, D. Kaiser, MD, "Commentary: Against Biologic Psychiatry," *Psychiatric Times* 13, no. 12 (1996).

6   *What struck me most about Rebecca's story*: CBS Broadcasting Inc. Documentary, *60 Minutes*: "What Killed Rebecca Riley?" 2007.

CHAPTER 1: BEYOND PSYCHIATRIC LABELS: WHAT STORIES TELL US

9   *an article in the* New York Times Magazine: J. Egan, "The Bipolar Puzzle," *New York Times Magazine*, Sept. 14, 2008.

11   *earned at least $1.6 million in consulting fees from drug companies*: G. Harris and B. Carey, "Researchers Fail to Reveal Full Drug Pay," *New York Times*, June 8, 2008.

11   *Colleagues of Dr. Biederman also received*: Ibid.

11   *Diller holds Biederman and his colleagues to be in part "morally responsible" for the death of Rebecca Riley*: L. Diller, MD, "Misguided Standards of Care," *Boston Globe*, June 19, 2007.

11   *"Dr. Biederman's work helped to fuel a fortyfold increase from 1994 to 2003 in the diagnosis of pediatric bipolar disorder"*: G. Harris, "Research Center Tied to Drug Company." *New York Times*, Nov. 24, 2008.

12   *some drug makers have resorted to intimidation*: Ibid.

12   *blacklisting of psychiatrists*: L. Diller, *The Last Normal Child* (Westport: Praeger, 2006) pp. 95ff.

13   *We accept the idea that politicians disguise spins as facts all the time*: B. Jackson and K. Jamieson, *Un-Spun: Finding Facts in a World of Disinformation* (New York: Random House, 2007).

13   *"Your mind is the strongest medicine"*: PBS, *The Tavis Smiley Show*, Dec. 25, 2008.

15   *Recent research with laboratory animals suggests that regular use of psycho-stimulants:* L. Sax, *Boys Adrift* (New York: Basic Books, 2007), pp. 89–91.

17   *between a quarter and half of the children at any given residential summer camp take psychiatric:* J. Gross, "Checklist for Camp: Bug Spray. Sunscreen. Pills," *New York Times,* July 16, 2006.

18   *regularly concealed by drug companies:* B. Carey and B. Meier, "Drug Maker Is Accused of Fraud." *New York Times,* Feb. 25, 2009.

22   *Ten years later, when Minuchin stepped down:* M. Nichols, *Family Therapy* (New York: Gardner Press, 1984), p. 471.

23   *A mother once consulted Erickson:* J. Haley, *Uncommon Therapy: The Psychiatric Techniques of Milton Erickson, M.D.* (New York: Norton, 1986).

24   *In family therapy research studies:* M. S. Robbins, J. Szapocznik, and V. E. Horigian, "Brief strategic family therapy for adolescents with behavior problems," in J. H. Bray (ed.) and M. Stanton, *Handbook of Family Psychology* (Oxford, United Kingdom: Wiley-Blackwell, 2009).

26   *Dorothy Bloch wrote touchingly:* D. Bloch, *So the Witch Won't Eat Me: Fantasy and the Child's Fear of Infanticide* (New York: Grove Press, 1984).

29   *Napier found this new way of seeing families:* A. Napier and C. Whitaker, *The Family Crucible* (New York: Bantam, 1978).

31   *Narrative therapists are interested in how society:* M. White and D. Epston, *Narrative Means to Therapeutic Ends* (New York: Norton, 1990).

CHAPTER 2: A NEW FRAME: STRATEGIC CHILD-FOCUSED FAMILY THERAPY

37   *Narrative therapists view psychiatric diagnoses as "trends":* M. White and D. Epston, *Narrative Means to Therapeutic Ends* (New York: Norton, 1990).

CHAPTER 3: LISTENING TO CHILDREN

63   *Salvador Minuchin reflected in a recent interview:* R. Simon, "From Revolution to Evolution," *Psychotherapy Networker* 33, no. 5 (2009): 52–55.

CHAPTER 4: METAPHOR

84   *A 1999 study by the U.S. Department of Health and Human Services:* NIMH, "Brief notes on the mental health of adolescents and children," 1999, http://www.medhelp.org/nihlib/GF-233.html.

98   *a technique called the "strategic dialogue" that I learned from the Italian strategic therapist Giorgio Nardone:* G. Nardone and A. Salvini, *The Strategic Dialogue* (London: Karnac Books Ltd., 2007).

CHAPTER 5: INVISIBLE ALLIANCES

106   *Donald Winnicott calls the imaginative world of children a "play space":* D. Winnicott, *Playing and Reality* (London: Tavistock Publications Limited, 1971).

109   *The strategic dialogue addresses the child at the level of perception and feeling:* G. Nardone and C. Portelli, *Knowing Through Changing: The Evolution of Brief Strategic Therapy* (Carmarthen: Crown, 2005).

113   *Salvador Minuchin calls the "signature arrangement of the troubled middle-class family":* S. Minuchin and M. Nichols, *Family Healing: Tales of Hope and Renewal from Family Therapy* (New York: Macmillan, 1993), p. 121.

123   *Estrangement and loneliness played a central part in the story of fifteen-year-old:*

This case was published in different form in M. Wedge, *In the Therapist's Mirror: Reality in the Making* (New York: Norton, 1996).

131 *In a fascinating case described by Salvador Minuchin*: S. Minuchin and M. Nichols, *Family Healing: Tales of Hope and Renewal from Family Therapy* (New York: Macmillan, 1993), pp. 115–44.

CHAPTER 6: READING BY NOT READING: THE POWER OF PARADOX

150 *was his intervention with a sixteen-year-old girl who sucked her thumb*: J. Haley, *Uncommon Therapy: The Psychiatric Techniques of Milton Erickson, M.D.* (New York: Norton, 1986), pp. 195–98.

151 *He writes compellingly about another patient of his, a seventh-grade boy who couldn't read*: Ibid., pp. 204–5.

153 *Helping young people with "resistant" parents*: Ibid., pp. 266ff.

CHAPTER 7: MEDICATION: THE PROMISE AND THE PERIL

161 *Psychologist Martha Stout*: M. Stout, *The Myth of Sanity: Divided Consciousness and the Promise of Awareness. Tales of Multiple Personality in Everyday Life* (New York: Penguin, 2001).

172 *As Minuchin has observed, when family sorrow*: S. Minuchin and M. Nichols, *Family Healing: Tales of Hope and Renewal from Family Therapy* (New York: Macmillan, 1993).

175 *One such family came to see me after their fourteen-year-old son*: This case was originally published in different form in M. Wedge, "The Al Qaeda Strategy," *Journal of Brief, Strategic and Systemic Therapies* 1, no. 1 (2007).

180 *Taffel argues that today's teens are "vertically challenged"*: R. Taffel, "Vertically Challenged," *Psychotherapy Networker* 33, no. 5 (2009): 22–57.

CHAPTER 8: THRESHOLD KIDS: A PASSAGE IN SEARCH OF A RITE

183 *bungee family*: The term "bungee family" comes from M. Strauss, "Bungee Families," *Psychotherapy Networker* 33, no. 5 (2009): 30–59.

186 *most "traditional" cultures, such as the Masai of Kenya, acknowledge that the passage from adolescence to adulthood is a painful and perilous life crisis*: A. Van Gennep, *The Rites of Passage: A Classic Study of Cultural Celebrations* (Chicago: University of Chicago Press, 1960).

186 *These rites of passage always include a ceremony for crossing the threshold, or limen*: Ibid., pp. 21ff.

186 *This transition to adulthood is guided by trusted older members of the community, who have a semi-magical status as participants in the ritual*: Ibid.

186 *Leonard Sax laments the lack of such traditions*: L. Sax, *Boys Adrift* (New York: Basic Books, 2007), pp. 166ff.

192 *This was the circumstance in one of Erickson's cases*: cited in J. Haley, *Uncommon Therapy: The Psychiatric Techniques of Milton Erickson, M.D.* (New York: Norton, 1986).

193 *Jay Haley admonishes therapists to persist with*: J. Haley, *Leaving Home* (New York: McGraw Hill, 1980).

194 *Haley urged family therapists to view*: Ibid.

195 *Haley describes an eighteen-year-old girl named Annabelle*: Ibid.

197 *Salvador Minuchin developed a unique strategy to get*: Ibid.

CHAPTER 9: FROM BIOLOGY TO BENEVOLENCE

203 *Autism researcher Simon Baron-Cohen reminds us that the Diagnostic and Statistical Manual*: S. Baron-Cohen, "The Short Life of a Diagnosis," *New York Times*, Nov. 9, 2009.

203 *"In psychiatry no one knows the causes of anything, so classification can be driven by all sorts of factors"—political, social, and financial*: Quoted in B. Carey, "Psychiatrists Revise the Book of Human Troubles," *New York Times*, Dec. 17, 2008.

204 *Gabrielle Carlson, director of child and adolescent psychiatry at Stony Brook School of Medicine, says*: Quoted in J. Egan, "The Bipolar Puzzle," *New York Times Magazine*, Sept. 14, 2008.

204 *dressing outlandishly and talking to strangers*: Ibid.

206 *According to one study*: L. Cosgrove, S. Krimsky, M. Vijayaraghaven, and L. Schneider, "Financial Ties Between DSM-IV Panel Members and the Pharmaceutical Industry," *Psychother Psychosom* 75, (2006): 154–60. The authors of the study write: "Of the 170 DSM panel members 95 (56%) had one or more financial associations with companies in the pharmaceutical industry. One hundred percent of the members of the panels on 'Mood Disorders' and 'Schizophrenia and Other Psychotic Disorders' had financial ties to drug companies . . . **Conclusions:** Our inquiry into the relationships between DSM panel members and the pharmaceutical industry demonstrates that there are strong financial ties between the industry and those who are responsible for developing and modifying the diagnostic criteria for mental illness."

206 *According to federally financed research by scientists at Columbia and Rutgers universities, children on Medicaid*: D. Wilson, "Poor Children Likelier to Get Antipsychotics," *New York Times*, Dec. 11, 2009.

207 *Medicaid provides antipsychotic drugs free of charge to covered children*: Ibid.

212 *because children "do not make the choice for themselves to take or not take a psychiatric drug"*: L. Diller, *The Last Normal Child: Essays on the Intersection of Kids, Culture, and Psychiatric Drugs* (Westport: Praeger, 2006), p. 14.

212 *Senator Charles Grassley, the ranking member on the Senate Finance Committee, has tenaciously pursued*: D. Wilson, "Senator Asks Pfizer About Harvard Payments," *New York Times*, March 3, 2009.

213 *"it must strip itself of false and hubristic claims"*: D. Kaiser, "Commentary: Against Biologic Psychiatry," *Psychiatric Times* 13, no. 12 (1996).

213 *A recently revealed trend is the drug industry's practice of using company employees to "ghostwrite" articles in respected medical journals*: S. Laidlaw, Medical ethics blog, June 12, 2009, http://thestar.blogs.com/ethics/2009/06/ghost writers-used-by-Lilly-to-promote-drugs-in-journals.html.

214 *According to Robert Whitaker*: R. Whitaker, *Mad in America: Bad Science, Bad Medicine, and the Enduring Mistreatment of the Mentally Ill* (New York: Basic Books, 2002), p. 28.

214 *Social historian Michel Foucault tells us*: M. Foucault, *Madness and Civilization: A History of Insanity in the Age of Reason* (New York: Vintage, 1988).

REFERENCES

Baron-Cohen, S. "The Short Life of a Diagnosis." *New York Times*, Nov. 9, 2009.

Bloch, D. *So the Witch Won't Eat Me: Fantasy and the Child's Fear of Infanticide*. New York: Grove Press, 1984.

Carey, B. "Debate Over Children and Psychiatric Drugs." *New York Times*, Feb. 15, 2007.

———. "Psychiatrists Revise the Book of Human Troubles." *New York Times*, Dec. 17, 2008.

Carey, B., and B. Meier. "Drug Maker Is Accused of Fraud." *New York Times*, Feb. 25, 2009.

Carey, B., and R. C. Rabin. "Study Finds Drug Risks with Newer Antipsychotics." *New York Times*, Jan. 14, 2009.

Castelnuevo, G. "Come Back to Hippocrates: The 'Forgotten' Principles in Mental Health." *Journal of Brief, Strategic & Systemic Therapies* 1, no. 1 (2007): 27–37.

CBS Broadcasting Inc. Documentary. *60 Minutes*: "What Killed Rebecca Riley?" 2007.

Cosgrove, L., S. Krimsky, M. Vijayaraghaven, and L. Schneider. "Financial Ties Between DSM-IV Panel Members and the Pharmaceutical Industry." *Psychother Psychosom* 75 (2006): 154–60.

Diller, L. *The Last Normal Child: Essays on the Intersection of Kids, Culture, and Psychiatric Drugs*. Westport: Praeger, 2006.

———. "Misguided Standards of Care." *Boston Globe*, June 19, 2007.

Egan, J. "The Bipolar Puzzle." *New York Times Magazine*, Sept. 14, 2008.

Foucault, M. *Madness and Civilization: A History of Insanity in the Age of Reason*. New York: Vintage, 1988.

Gross, J. "Checklist for Camp: Bug Spray. Sunscreen. Pills." *New York Times*, July 16, 2006.

Haley, J. *Problem-Solving Therapy*. New York: Harper, 1976.

————. *Leaving Home*. New York: McGraw-Hill, 1980.

————. *Uncommon Therapy: The Psychiatric Techniques of Milton Erickson, M.D.* New York: Norton, 1986.

Haley, J., and B. Montalvo. "In Defense of Child Therapy." *Family Process*, 1973.

Harris, G. "Research Center Tied to Drug Company." *New York Times*, Nov. 24, 2008.

————. "Drug Maker Told Studies Would Aid It, Papers Say." *New York Times*, March 19, 2009.

Harris, G., and B. Carey. "Researchers Fail to Reveal Full Drug Pay." *New York Times*, June 8, 2008.

Himaras, E. "Rebecca's Agony: Her Last Seven Days." *Patriot Ledger*, Oct. 28, 2008.

Isaacs, M., B. Montalvo, and D. Abelsohn. *The Difficult Divorce*. New York: Basic Books, 1986.

Jackson, B., and K. Jamieson. *Un-Spun: Finding Facts in a World of Disinformation*. New York: Random House, 2007.

Kaiser, D., MD. "Commentary: Against Biologic Psychiatry." *Psychiatric Times* 13, no. 12 (1996).

Kolata, G. "Boom in Ritalin Sales Raises Ethical Issues." *New York Times*, May 15, 1996.

Laidlaw, S. Medical ethics blog. June 12, 2009. http://thestar.blogs.com/ethics/2009/06/ghostwriters-used-by-Lilly-to-promote-drugs-in-journals.html.

Minuchin, S., and Michael P. Nichols. *Family Healing: Tales of Hope and Renewal from Family Therapy*. New York: Macmillan, 1993.

Mosher, L., MD. "Soteria and Other Alternatives to Acute Psychiatric Hospitalization: A Personal and Professional Review." *Journal of Nervous and Mental Disease* 187 (1999): 142–49.

Napier, A., and C. Whitaker. *The Family Crucible*. New York: Bantam, 1978.

Nardone, G., and C. Portelli. *Knowing Through Changing: The Evolution of Brief Strategic Therapy*. Carmarthen: Crown, 2005.

Nardone, G., and A. Salvini. *The Strategic Dialogue*. London: Karnac Books Ltd., 2007.

Nichols, M. *Family Therapy*. New York: Gardner Press, 1984.

NIMH. "Brief notes on the mental health of adolescents and children." 1999. http://www.medhelp.org/nihlib/GF-233.html.

Pediatrics 123, no. 2 (Feb. 2009).

Phelps, M. (2008). *No Limits: The Will to Succeed*. New York: Free Press, 2008.

Pies, R., MD. "Redefining Depression as Mere Sadness." *New York Times*, Sept. 17, 2008.

Robbins, M. S., J. Szapocznik, and V. E. Horigian. "Brief strategic family therapy for adolescents with behavior problems." In J. H. Bray (ed.) and M. Stanton, *Handbook of Family Psychology*. Oxford, United Kingdom: Wiley-Blackwell, 2009.

Sax, L., MD, PhD. *Boys Adrift*. New York: Basic Books, 2007.

Selvini Palazzoli, M., L. Boscolo, G. Cecchin, and G. Prata. *Paradox and Counterparadox: A New Model in the Therapy of the Family in Schizophrenic Transaction*. New York: Jason Aronson, 1978.

Simon, R. "From Revolution to Evolution." *Psychotherapy Networker* 33, no. 5 (2009): 52–55.

Stout, M. *The Myth of Sanity: Divided Consciousness and the Promise of Awareness. Tales of Multiple Personality in Everyday Life.* New York: Penguin, 2001.

Strauss, M. "Bungee Families." *Psychotherapy Networker* 33, no. 5 (2009): 30–59.

Taffel, R. (2009). "Vertically Challenged." *Psychotherapy Networker* 33, no. 5 (2009): 22–57.

Turner, V. *The Ritual Process.* New York: De Gruyter, 1969.

Van Gennep, A. *The Rites of Passage: A Classic Study of Cultural Celebrations.* Chicago: University of Chicago Press, 1960.

Warner, J. "Why Rebecca Died." *New York Times*, Feb. 22, 2007.

Wedge, M. *In the Therapist's Mirror: Reality in the Making.* New York: Norton, 1996.

———. "The Al Qaeda Strategy." *Journal of Brief, Strategic and Systemic Therapies* 1, no. 1 (2007).

Whitaker, R. *Mad in America: Bad Science, Bad Medicine, and the Enduring Mistreatment of the Mentally Ill.* New York: Basic Books, 2002.

White, M., and D. Epston. *Narrative Means to Therapeutic Ends.* New York: Norton, 1990.

Wilson, D. "Harvard Medical School in Ethics Quandary." *New York Times*, March 2, 2009.

———. "Senator Asks Pfizer About Harvard Payments." *New York Times*, March 3, 2009.

———. "Poor Children Likelier to Get Antipsychotics." *New York Times*, Dec. 11, 2009.

Winnicott, D. *Playing and Reality.* London: Tavistock Publications Limited, 1971.

INDEX

Marilyn Wedge, PhD, MFT, is a family therapist in private practice with more than twenty years of experience working with children, adolescents, and families. She has a doctorate from the University of Chicago, where she was a Danforth Foundation Scholar, and did a postdoctoral fellowship at the Hastings Center for Bioethics. She has taught at the California State University, East Bay; the College of the Art Institute of Chicago; and the Chicago YMCA Community College. She is the author of two books and several articles on family therapy and has presented her work at many professional conferences. She has three children and one grandchild and lives in Oak Park, California, with her husband, Gene.